Classroom Practices in Teaching English 1980–1981

371.9
D 279s

Classroom Practices
in Teaching English
1980–1981

Dealing with Differences

Gene Stanford, Chair,
and the Committee on Classroom Practices

National Council of Teachers of English
1111 Kenyon Road, Urbana, Illinois 61801

Grateful acknowledgment is made for permission to reprint the following material: "Teaching Gay Students," reprinted with permission from *Change* Magazine, Vol. 9, No. 5 (May 1977). Copyrighted by the Council on Learning, 271 North Avenue, New Rochelle, N.Y. 10801. "This Is Just to Say," from *Collected Earlier Poems* of William Carlos Williams. Copyright 1938 by New Directions Publishing Corporation. Reprinted by permission of New Directions. "Vacation" from *Stories That Could Be True* by William Stafford. Copyright © 1960 by William Stafford. Reprinted by permission of Harper & Row, Publishers, Inc. "Caring and Curriculum for 'Special' Students" and "Failure Is No Fun—A Competency-Based Approach That Generates Success," reprinted from *Connecticut English Journal.* "The Good News about Newspapers," reprinted from *The Journal of Reading*, Vol. 24, No. 3. Copyrighted by the International Reading Association. Reprinted with permission of Chip Shields, Linda Vondrak and the International Reading Association.

It is the policy of NCTE in its journals and other publications to provide a forum for the open discussion of ideas concerning the content and the teaching of English and the language arts. Publicity accorded to any particular point of view does not imply endorsement by the Executive Committee, the Board of Directors, or the membership at large, except in announcements of policy where such endorsement is clearly specified.

Library of Congress Cataloging in Publication Data

Main entry under title:

Dealing with differences.

  (Classroom practices in teaching English ; 1980–1981)
  Includes bibliographies.
  1. Exceptional children—Education—Language arts—Addresses, essays, lectures.   2. English language—Study and teaching (Secondary)—Addresses, essays, lectures.   3. Mainstreaming in education —Addresses, essays, lectures.   I. Stanford, Gene. II. National Council of Teachers of English. Committee on Classroom Practices.   III. Series.
LC3973.D4   371.9′046   80-25014
ISBN 0-8141-0690-0

Contents

Preface

The search for specific ways to deal with students who have special needs was the dominant theme of the open meeting of the Committee on Classroom Practices in Teaching English, held in San Francisco on November 22, 1979. Four members of the Council joined the five committee members in responding to the question, "What are the pressing issues facing English teachers today?" The discussion returned again and again to the problem of increasing numbers of exceptional students with whom the teacher must deal: physically, emotionally, and mentally handicapped; non-native speakers; nontraditional students; speakers of nonstandard dialects; the gifted and talented; and alienated, disenchanted, and unmotivated learners. The committee soon realized that virtually all concerns expressed could be addressed in the 1980 publication with a focus on "Dealing with Differences in the English Classroom."

Promptly after the meeting, invitations for manuscripts on teaching special students were issued in *Language Arts, English Journal, Council-Grams, College English,* and *English Education,* and in the journals of numerous NCTE-affiliated organizations.

By the April 15 deadline, 101 manuscripts were submitted by educators in 31 states, the District of Columbia, Canada, and the People's Republic of China. The manuscripts, with authors' names removed, were evaluated by committee members Jean Procope-Martin, Jeffrey N. Golub, Raymond J. Rodrigues, and the Chair—a committee representing different geographic areas and a variety of viewpoints at several educational levels.

Twenty-four manuscripts—written by educators at all levels of the educational system—were ultimately selected for publication and approved by the Council's Editorial Board. They address the needs of students as diverse as the geographical regions and educational settings in which their authors work, and reveal a deep commitment by members of the profession to reach all students, regardless of how they may diverge from what is believed to be "typical."

Introduction

When Eli Whitney invented the assembly line process of manufacturing he designed it for making rifles, not educating children. But at some point the idea seems to have crept into the minds of the American public that what is good for the Model T must be good for American students. And over recent decades, American schools have come to function more and more like assembly lines, with inputs and outputs and quality controls—and rejects.

In recent years, lawmakers, at the same time when they were demanding more rigid enforcement of assembly line techniques in the schools—such as performance objectives and competency tests—threw a monkey wrench into the production line. They mandated "mainstreaming" of students who previously were thought to require separate and special education. The Education for All Handicapped Children Act (P.L. 94-142) mandated that the stream of regular classroom instruction be enlarged to accommodate children with special learning problems. The law established their right to an appropriate education in the least restrictive environment possible. This did not mean, however, that handicapped children or others with special problems should be dumped into regular classes with untrained teachers, as some districts have done to save money. Rather, the law required that an individualized educational plan be drawn up for each child in consultation with the parents.

No Detroit automaker would attempt to build Cadillacs or Cordobas on an assembly line designed for Fords. But that is exactly what teachers are expected to do. All the students who do not fit on the assembly line—the geniuses and the handicapped, the very creative and the very dull—must be shoved right back into the 30-student/40-minute/uniform-test-at-the-end assembly line. And it isn't working!

Teachers facing this problem have had several choices. Unfortunately, the simplest solution might be to quietly sabotage the plan. The geniuses can easily be provoked into becoming discipline problems—and then suspended. The dull can be flunked until they drop out from frustration. The handicapped can be ridiculed or ignored until they stay home or at least become invisible. And the assembly line can grind inexorably on.

But to their credit most teachers have looked for a better way out of the dilemma. As exemplified by the contributors to this volume, they have adopted a different strategy: Reject the assembly line instead of the students. They have sought, devised, and implemented a myriad of approaches that take into account a principle that we seem to need reminding of repeatedly: Learners are not all alike, and we can expect them to succeed only if our planning takes these differences into account.

The differences are most apparent, of course, when students have obvious physical handicaps, such as blindness or deafness. But other impediments may need just as much of the teacher's concern and creativity—shyness, low intellectual ability, poor reading skills. Even being a generation older than most others in the class can be a liability unless the instructor is willing to acknowledge the difference and devise ways to bridge the gap between age groups.

Students' differences are not always synonymous with deficiencies. As many contributors to this volume have realized, assembly line education is as ill-suited to bright and creative students as it is to slow learners. They need educational experiences that challenge their ability and stimulate their creativity. Yet, at the same time, many of us are struck by the fact that many learning experiences created with gifted students in mind are potentially useful with students of other ability levels. As Sheila A. Lisman "confesses" in the final article in this volume, her strategy for teaching poetry to gifted students intrigued other, more nearly "average" students, and she used the same idea successfully with a variety of other classes. Her discovery is yet another reminder that we must look beyond the label affixed to a group of students and instead offer the best learning experiences we can devise to the individuals who make up that group.

With the new laws that return exceptional students to the regular classroom, with the recent enrollment in our schools of new groups of non-native speakers of English, with our continued concern for the special needs of minority students, we may at last discover that each learner is unique, that all students are "different" in ways that should influence how we teach them. If so, we will be able to forget the labels and truly individualize our instruction. We can then create new models of education which respect differences and demonstrate that quality, not uniformity, is still a possibility in American education. There can be no more worthy aspiration for the profession in a year bearing the Presidential Theme, "Unity in Diversity."

Gene Stanford
Chair

1 Responses to Mainstreaming

Handicapped, Yes, but Not in the English Class

Pamela J. Mills
Raymond J. Rodrigues
University of Colorado

Recent changes in the law, in particular the Education of Handicapped Children's Act of 1975 (P.L. 94-142), have increased the number of "atypical" students in regular high school classes. Although once encouraged to drop out of school as soon as legally possible, students with differences now have the legislative and judicial impetus both for remaining in school and for insisting on instruction that will enable them to learn to their capacity. Teachers at all levels of the continuum have been told that *all* students, handicapped or not, have a right to a free, appropriate public education in the least restrictive environment. At the high school level, due to the importance of the content area, English teachers are now facing an ever increasing number and variety of students with educational differences, differences that make additional demands on high school English teachers' skills.

In order to integrate handicapped students within the regular English classroom, teachers must develop ways to reduce the defeat and frustration normally accompanying instruction of the handicapped in the regular classroom and to increase the students' self-concepts by reducing failure and improving the students' competencies. The handicapped students most likely to be integrated into the regular high school English classroom are those with mild and moderate learning problems, including the learning disabled, the emotionally disturbed and the mentally retarded, those with sensory impairments of hearing and sight, and those with a variety of physical handicaps. Depending upon the specific types of handicaps they encounter, teachers will be faced with the challenge of examining the adequacy of curricular content, altering teaching strategies, and modifying teaching materials and the physical environment (Mills, 1979). In particular, teaching strategies must be used which match the "individual learning styles, capacities and interests of the students with learning problems" (Lexington Teacher Training Project, 1974, p. 3) with the abilities of the teachers who instruct these students.

3

Curricular Content

Before even attempting to teach handicapped students within their class-rooms, English teachers must first determine what content in the regular curriculum is appropriate and necessary for these students to learn and, second, develop approaches based upon the specific nature and degree of the handicapping condition. For the mentally retarded student, the teacher must ask what is essential for the student to know in order to get along in society. This will depend largely upon the degree of retardation and current functioning level, but most of the regular content may not be necessary for this student.

For the learning disabled or emotionally disturbed student, the teacher must find ways for the student to compensate for the handicapping condition while demanding high standards of performance. The students must be taught to use their academic and behavioral strengths to override the deficiencies inherent within their handicaps. Altering instructional strategies and materials will usually allow even the most severely disabled student to benefit from instruction.

For the deaf or hard-of-hearing student, the age at which the loss occurred, the degree of hearing loss, and the language ability of the student will, to a large extent, determine the content that should be taught. Since many aspects of the language arts will cause difficulties for the hearing impaired student (Gearheart and Weishahn, 1976), English teachers must be prepared to examine their curriculum and to teach according to the language level of the student. Students with hearing deficits should be encouraged to use whatever hearing they have, to watch closely the person speaking (speechread), and to speak in complete sentences. Students should not be allowed to get by with only a yes/no answer or with incomplete sentences.

The blind or partially sighted student will probably require little if any alteration in the curriculum, but will require alterations in teaching strategies and materials. This should also be true of many physically handicapped students, depending upon the specific limitations imposed.

General guidelines to use for adapting or modifying the English curriculum to meet the needs of the handicapped student include:

1. *Don't lower standards, but demand excellence at appropriate levels.* A blind student, for example, cannot be expected to read regular print for comprehension, but that same student can listen to a story or poem read aloud and can often exhibit memory skills that most students with normal vision have not attained. Therefore, asking some students to read to the blind student can provide sighted students with practice in reading

while giving the visually handicapped student practice in listening and, most importantly, giving both of them practice in developing their comprehension.

Even though a physically handicapped student may not be able to manipulate a pencil or pen, that student may be able to speak, and in that manner dictate to another student or into a tape recorder. Composing orally is a skill that many speech teachers stress, but one that is often ignored in the English classroom.

2. *Reduce the amount to be done, not the level to be accepted.* A student can demonstrate knowledge of the basic components of an essay by writing one-paragraph introductions, conclusions, and bodies. The requirement to write 500 words will not elicit five times more knowledge than will a 100-word assignment. Similarly, a teacher can ascertain a student's knowledge of formal research paper components by limiting the number of examples required. While the nonhandicapped student may indeed demonstrate greater linguistic flexibility through having to produce in quantity, we have no proof that demanding quantity leads to greater fluency.

3. *Don't expect students to be able to demonstrate their skills only in written tests.* So much of what occurs in a classroom is oral; however, for some reason, evaluation in English classes tends to take place almost exclusively in writing. Consider the following variations as perfectly valid evaluation procedures:

a. To demonstrate an understanding of a play, perform a segment of that play for the rest of the class. Perform it in a way that shows understanding of the character's motivation and the author's intentions.

b. Take tests together. The student who can write may do the actual writing while the other student acts as a resource, a devil's advocate, or a clarifier.

c. Evaluate and respond to a piece of literature in a one-to-one conference with the teacher.

d. Debate an issue raised by a reading in the class.

e. Prepare an oral interpretation for the class. Comprehension should be revealed by the clarity and appropriateness of delivery.

Teaching Strategies

Although many of the handicapped students in regular classrooms can learn through normal instruction, some will require that modifications be made in the way instruction is provided. Handicapped and "normal" students alike may benefit from the following:

1. *Individualized instruction with the teacher working as a resource for students.* Students need not always perform in front of an entire class. Those students who are sensitive about their handicaps may be inhibited by public recitations. At the same time, if they are the only ones given individual projects, they may feel insulted. By increasing the individualization of the entire class, the teacher can enable the handicapped students to feel that they belong, rather than that they are once again being singled out.

Individualized reading programs often stimulate all students to read more because they can select topics they are interested in. Student writing assignments can be tailored to their abilities and levels of achievement. Writing improvement occurs most often when the students' own writings are used as the text, when students write about subjects they know best, and when there is a valid reason for students to write, such as for publication. The only persons that students need to compete with are themselves—their past performances used to establish goals for their future performances.

2. *Small group instruction.* By employing flexible grouping strategies, teachers can work with students having similar problems. Students whose compositions—oral or written—reveal weak organization patterns can work together to improve them. Sentence-combining activities aimed at developing students' abilities to employ, for example, subordinate clauses at the beginnings of sentences need only be used with those students who need such training. Students whose handicaps interfere with their demonstrating English language abilities can be placed in short-term groups for special training. Or, if a teacher assigns different members of groups specific and separate tasks that relate to the central purpose of the group, then handicapped members of the group can be given tasks they can accomplish, thereby making their contributions important ones.

3. *Peer tutoring.* One truism reveals that one learns best when one has to teach something. Therefore, tutoring is valuable for both the tutor and the person tutored. While peer tutors work with special students, the rest of the class can continue to operate in a regular fashion, and the tutor can receive credit for the tutoring.

The teacher can prepare a series of directed study guides, with clearly stated objectives, procedures, and materials for the tutor. If a composition is to be evaluated, for example, the teacher can give the tutor a list of key questions to ask about the composition and instructions on how to guide the special student through the evaluation. These study guides and materials can be stored in envelopes, file folders, or even shoe boxes for easy access.

4. *Oral vs. written instruction.* Here, the teacher might best consider both possibilities. A student who cannot comprehend rapid speech can be given written instructions. A student who cannot deal with written material can be given oral instructions. If a class has students requiring both kinds of instruction, the teacher can make it a practice to give instructions in several ways.

5. *Self-correcting materials and tests.* The more handicapped students a teacher has in class, the more likely it is that those students are at different levels of development. Therefore, mechanical matters, such as vocabulary study, skills development in mechanics, and syntactic exercises should be structured so that students can correct their own work and keep track of their own progress. This helps eliminate the frustration of competing with others in the class and helps students develop at their own pace. Full class sessions can then be devoted to such activities as literature discussions, creative drama presentations, and media events.

6. *Students select their own groups or work individually.* To say that all special students would prefer to work in groups or individually would be misleading. Therefore, students should, when possible, be given the choice of either approach. Every student in the class should be given those choices, not just the handicapped students. Some composition assignments, for example, benefit from the input of many authors. Others, especially those that are highly personal, are best produced by individuals.

7. *Minimized reading and rule memorization.* As we have noted, the quantity of work may have to be adjusted to match the capabilities of special students. Shorter reading selections for some students and limited or no rule memorization for others may enable them to survive in the regular classroom. The latter provides us with one more reason to avoid teaching grammatical terminology out of the context of a student's composition, that practice having been repeatedly shown to be ineffective in improving composition skills.

8. *Contracts.* If a teacher manages a class by contract, all of the teaching strategy variations mentioned can be built into contracts. For special students, the contract allows choices that enable them to pick ways to succeed. In such cases, the choices should truly be those of the students, not the teacher. Often, a special student may want to attempt a task the teacher considers too difficult, but the student's desire to overcome the handicap may be the best thing that could happen.

Special Teaching Materials

Most of the materials normally used in the regular classroom can be readily adapted to meet the needs of the handicapped students. By merely matching the kind of learning required by a specific material with the learning abilities of the students, teachers can increase the potential of all students to learn. In addition, some other adaptations might be required:

1. *Large-print materials.* If a teacher has visually impaired students in the classroom, materials typed with a primary or other kind of large-print typewriter may help those students read handouts more easily. In addition, the school should order large-print copies of texts and literature selections whenever available. Even if the handicapped student is not reading the same selections as other students, the student is at least reading. In fact, having such students in the classroom may be just the impetus for developing an individualized reading program.

2. *Reduced vocabulary level and texts on different levels.* For students whose mental abilities do not allow them to perform equally with other students, teachers should provide alternative reading assignments. And in giving assignments and instructions, teachers should always consider their particular selection of vocabulary. Some students may not be able to handle complex vocabulary and concepts, but if, for instance, the class is studying the novel, students who cannot handle complex novels can certainly handle less complex ones. The main point is that they are encountering and responding to novels.

3. *Tape recorders.* Tape recorders have multiple uses in classes with special students. Students can compose into tape recorders and teachers can evaluate individual work on tape recorders. Students who have difficulty speaking can speak into the tape recorder and can ask questions in an atmosphere less pressured than the classroom. Using cassette recorders, teachers can give assignments to students who need more time to assimilate and think about assignments. Providing each student in the class with a cassette tape is a minimal expenditure that can result in many classroom uses.

Classroom Environment

Common sense can often be the guide for determing the environmental modifications required by specific handicaps. Free seating and the use of study carrels are usually beneficial for many students, including those without identifiable handicaps. Allowing the students themselves to determine the adaptations required will often suffice, and minor adjustments may be the only alterations required.

The handicapped student in the regular English classroom may require some modification of what is "normal." By first determining the appropriate curricular content, then altering the teaching strategies and carefully choosing the special teaching materials, the regular class teacher can help ensure the success of the handicapped learner. Modifying the curriculum, methods, materials, and environment to meet the needs of special students may enhance the learning for all students.

References

Gearheart, B.R., and Weishahn, M.W. *The Handicapped Child in the Regular Classroom*. St. Louis: C.V. Mosby Co., 1976.

Lexington Teacher Training Project. *Every Student Is Different: The High School*. Lexington, Mass.: Lexington Public Schools, 1974.

Mills, P.J. "Adapting the Regular Classroom to Meet Special Needs." *Teaching-Learning Review*, 1979, *1* (2), 16–18.

Weiss, H.G., and Weiss, M.S. *A Survival Manual: Case Studies and Suggestions for the Learning Disabled Teenager*. Great Barrington, Mass.: Treehouse Associates, 1976.

Caring and Curriculum for "Special" Students

Patricia Phelan
Morse High School, San Diego

"Mainstreaming of handicapped students" raises fears and uncertainties for the regular classroom teacher. What does "handicapped" mean and what behaviors should the teacher expect from these students? What is the best way to meet the needs of all students in the room when "handicapped" students are a part of the group? What kinds of language arts experiences can be offered to assist all students in gaining an awareness of the needs and experiences which both "handicapped" and "regular" people share in common? This paper will suggest three ways to meet students' needs: 1) Create an atmosphere of caring in the room and maintain a matter-of-fact teacher attitude. 2) Offer a variety of learning experiences so that a wide range of student interests will be tapped. 3) Take good care of yourself as a teacher so that you will have the resilience to be open to the needs of others.

The Caring Classroom

Mainstreaming handicapped students means that there will be students in your classes now who have been in special classes before. These young people may have such disabilities as hearing impairment, orthopedic problems, impaired vision, emotional handicaps, all of the things which keep them from performing as well as the average student. Often these disabilities are physically obvious. In such cases the student's need is easy to perceive because the difference is readily apparent. One way to help everyone get along together is to create an atmosphere of "caring" in the classroom. When students having special needs are first placed in your room, there may be surprises and difficulties, but overall it can be a rich experience, both for you and for all of the class. A student with a particular physical handicap often has something of special value to offer others because she has had more time for introspection and observation, may know herself better, may understand others better because she understands herself.

You can create a "caring" atmosphere by encouraging activities which will help students become better acquainted (Fader, 1976). Have them write notes to each other; write letters of introduction; write letters in which all of the information they tell about themselves is a lie; write under assumed names; introduce each other aloud; make collage posters which represent them and their interests. Structure assignments so that students move around the room and get a chance to meet each other until all of them know one another on a first name basis.

As the teacher, stand at the door and greet each person coming into the room. Exchange notes with students as your time permits. Be a question-asker and a listener to find out what students care about. Form and re-form small groups for peer evaluation of writing, as in read-arounds of letters and compositions, so that students share a wide range of ideas with many people. Arrange discussions on topics related to reading and writing so that ideas are shared verbally. (See teaching suggestions, which follow in Curriculum Variety section.)

A caring atmosphere will show all of the students in the room that they are important as individuals, that they matter to you, and that their support of each other will be a continuing benefit to them in the learning enterprise. After the first few days of having handicapped students in your class, it will become clear that you are all the same—just people in a room together, enjoying each other, working, learning, being happy or cranky or sleepy. I have found that it reassures the class if I am fairly matter-of-fact and relaxed about a special student.

Often it is difficult to show your concern and affection for a person by being calm and friendly yet firm in your expectation that this student will do his best work, that this student will do what he knows is best for himself. Though in the past a handicapped student may be used to special treatment in a special class, most students do not really want special favors; they want to be accepted as full, capable human beings. I do not aim to "rescue" needy students in Karpman's sense of helping them to do things they can and prefer to do for themselves (Karpman, 1968). I do aim to provide a safe, comfortable, caring, academic setting. When not sure what to do, simply ask the student if she wants your help. Better yet, wait; let her take care of the problem in her own way or seek your assistance.

One word about the "needy" student. It is usually clear who the handicapped students are when they come to your class. It is not always so easy to notice the special needs of students who are already part of the class. Some needs are frequently hidden, like family break-ups, depression, psychological or physical battering. As teachers we do not have to agree on definitions of "needy," "normal," "abnormal," or "handicapped" in order to deal effectively with all of our students. As young people practice caring for one another in a more cooperative than competitive setting, under the leadership of a teacher who exhibits a matter-of-fact attitude toward each student, the needs of all will be more adequately met.

Curriculum Variety

Offer a wide range of language arts learning experiences so that all students can find success in a variety of ways. When a handicapped student is assigned to your room, simply treat him like any other student until you are acquainted. If you are uncomfortable at the thought of having handicapped students in your classroom, check with the Resource Specialist who is planning the IEPs (Individualized Education Programs) for these youngsters, in order to find out more about each person. The expert will know a lot about individuals, but it is important to remember that *you* are the only expert available when it comes to teaching your subject in your classroom. A Resource Specialist can give advice about teaching a small group in a special class; at the same time, you already know enough to do the same fine job of teaching that you are already doing with your classes. Sometimes the formal academic records of a student, in combination with past classroom performance which falls short of that student's potential, will indicate to you that you should not expect *too* much. This may be a mistake, so create a mood of acceptance and caring for the whole class, then wait to see what the special needs of your mainstreamed students may be.

Students with obvious physical handicaps *may* work a bit slower, *may* need more explanation, *may* be short-tempered. Having said this much, I think it is a mistake to make such statements at all, because each person is an individual. Each handicapped student in my room has been entirely unique in needs, abilities, attitudes and personality. If, however, more time *is* needed to complete assignments or there is physical difficulty in doing the work at all, here are some classroom procedures which may prove useful:

1. In a caring room, everyone is a potential teacher. Students can serve as secretaries or assistants to teach others. This is a good bridge between being uneasy and becoming comfortable; as soon as possible, the handicapped student should do all of her own work.

2. Tape recorders are useful for listening to stories recorded ahead of time or for recording compositions which a person cannot write but can talk out loud. Typewriters are useful for someone who cannot write easily.

3. Appeal to a variety of senses in assignments, not just to help the

handicapped, but also to widen experience for the average student and provide alternative hemisphere modes of thinking (Phelan, 1978).

4. Music adds a great deal to literature. For example, "He Ain't Heavy; He's My Brother," a song by Neil Diamond, expresses the caring mood well. Ask the students to bring in music which represents ideas under discussion in class.

5. Film, filmmaking, slides—visual literacy in all its forms offers students a chance to experience the composing process in different ways.

While planning your language arts activities, it is useful to remember that everyone in the room, teacher included, wants to learn. As John Holt (1969) puts it,

> Every child, without exception, has an innate and unquenchable drive to understand the world in which he lives and to gain freedom and competence in it. Whatever truly adds to his understanding, his capacity for growth and pleasure, his powers, his sense of his own freedom, dignity and worth may be said to be true education.

This is one guide which will help you to sort out your teaching objectives and keep those which truly affirm a student's sense of freedom, dignity, and worth.

One way to assist students in learning more about the world, is to provide opportunities to see, hear, talk, write, and think about new ideas. Any good book will offer this possibility, a chance to enter into the life space and *be* someone else for a while—living, experiencing, making decisions, and having to live with the results of those decisions. At this point, you will have to make a decision about the type of book to use. If your class has no "special" students in it right now and you want to widen their understanding of special needs through fine books on the subject, choose some from the list below. All of the titles included have been enjoyed by both junior and senior high school students.

Some Books Dealing with Specific Handicaps

Jones, Ron. *The Acorn People*—a true story about a group of seriously handicapped young people who attend summer camp and win many personal victories in their struggles.

Kaufman, Barry. *Son-Rise*—when their infant son is diagnosed as an autistic child, a family unites its forces to win the boy back to the real world. (true story)

Kerr, M. E. *Dinky Hocker Shoots Smack*—a lonely girl turns to compulsive eating in order to quiet her feeling of loneliness.

Mazer, Harry. *The War on Villa Street*—a junior high boy copes with his alcoholic father and befriends a mentally retarded classmate.

Sherburne, Zoa. *Why Have the Birds Stopped Singing?*—a high school girl with epilepsy travels into her family past and meets a distant relative, similarly afflicted, many years ago.

If you already have some handicapped students in class and feel that the books mentioned may prove depressing or heavy for the class, I suggest that everyone would enjoy reading *The Boy Who Could Make Himself Disappear*, by Kin Platt. The book has been rendered into a movie, *Baxter*, which is an excellent film if you can find it available in your area.

Whatever books you choose, whether one book for the class or individual choice, here are some questions and activities which will help students to think about the book they are reading.

Questions to Consider during or after the Reading:

1. What is the handicap *every* person in the story has to face? For example, in *The Boy Who Could Make Himself Disappear*, Roger, his mother, his father, Dr. Clemm, every other character has certain "handicaps" which get in the way of living fully in the world.

2. How does this handicap affect *each* person's ability to deal effectively with the real world?

3. What is the outcome of the conflict in the story? What do you think will happen next? What is the author mainly telling you about human beings and living? Do you agree? Why or why not?

4. Compare or contrast characters/events in the story with someone or some happening in your own experience.

5. What do you want to remember of your life fifty years from now? How do you want to *be* remembered? For example, "I want to be remembered as a person who is . . ." [a certain quality], or "I want to be remembered as a person who . . ." [does certain things, actions].

Activities to Do during or after the Reading:

1. Make a filmstrip illustrating key events in the book or make a storyboard to illustrate an important scene.

2. Bring in and play for the class a musical selection to go along with the book. If there are lyrics, plan ahead so copies can be duplicated

and shared for everyone to follow along while listening. Be ready to tell how this is related to your story.

3. Mold a clay figure, head, symbol from the story.

4. Make a collage to illustrate the significant ideas, happenings, or characters in the story.

5. Write a letter to one of the characters; write a letter to a movie or TV producer casting the actors for the production and describing the opening shot.

6. Change the ending; how did you change it? Why? How is this new ending more satisfactory to you than the one in the book?

7. Make a time line of the story, putting in all of the major events; make a time line for one of the characters in the story. Include some past and future as you imagine it might be if these are not provided in the book. Make a time line of your own life to place beside the one you make for the book person.

8. Assume the role of one of the characters in the book. Write a letter, a note, or a list to another character within the same book, to someone in your real world, to a character in another book. Use some of your own feelings and experiences.

9. As a class first, then as an individual, do a "cluster" or a word association about one main idea from a book (some ideas are "Striving," "Success," "Fear," "Friendship," "Alcohol," "Independence," "Love," "Loneliness"). Put the word or idea in the middle and then write any ideas that come to you, connecting them. Turn this into a prose selection when you find a string of ideas that you want to put together and express (Rico, n.d.). For example, while reading *The Boy Who Could Make Himself Disappear* I might express "Kindness" with this cluster of associations as a prewriting experience:

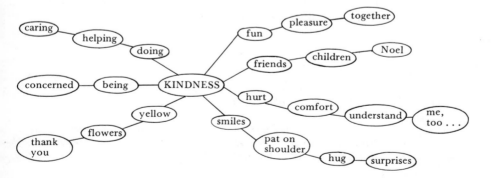

Mainstreaming of handicapped students into the regular English classroom offers us a chance to experience the richness, variety, creativity of all being human beings together.

Caring for Yourself

Caring for myself as a teacher-person is essential if I am to have that calm, relaxed manner which reassures students. How do *you* keep yourself sane in this profession? Experts write about the individual needs of students, but little is written about teachers' needs. Consider one of your average teaching days—the paper work, 150 to 175 different students who come through your life, other teachers you meet, committees and meetings after school, preparations. And then you go HOME. A leading psychologist once said that every ten minutes we need to have something to look forward to. Each day must include something in it that meets your own needs: music, quiet, a little pleasure reading, a movie, some pleasant conversation. Maybe it will only be a few minutes. How about half an hour in the park or over an after dinner cup of coffee in a nearby cafe? Dishes, shopping, and schoolwork will wait while you take care of yourself. Make a fun list of fifty things you love to do, and do one every day. Plan ahead for those one or two day mini-vacations which so refresh the spirit. Make yourself a Stroke Box (an old stationery box with a plastic see-through lid) in which you place notes, letters, mementos from good friends and times. Everytime you open your desk drawer at school, you'll see this collection of affirmations and smile. Keep one at home, too. On gloomy days open and read all those strokes. They are instant vitamins for the spirit. Remember, you are the "significant other" person in many lives every day, and *you* deserve special care, too.

Creating the caring classroom, offering activities which expand your horizons, and caring for yourself as a teacher/person are some ways of coping with this new educational experience.

References

Fader, Daniel. *The New Hooked on Books*. New York: Berkley Publishing Corp., 1976.

Karpman, Steve. "Fairy Tales and Script Drama Analysis." *Transactional Analysis Bulletin*, 7 (April 1968). Or Muriel James and Dorothy Jongeward. *Born to Win*. Menlo Park: Addison-Wesley, 1971.

Phelan, Patricia. "Right Brain/Left Brain: An Individual Learning Project Demonstrating How to Double Thinking Power by Using Both Hemispheres of the Brain." Lakeside, Calif.: *Interact,* 1978.

Holt, John. *The Underachieving School.* New York: Dell Publishing Co., 1969.

Rico, Gabriele. "Metaphor, Cognition, and Clustering." Abstract from School of Humanities and the Arts publication, University of California, San Jose.

Class-Mating: A Strategy for Teaching Writing in Urban Schools

James L. Collins
State University of New York at Buffalo

The urban secondary English classroom is truly a pluralistic community, and pluralism creates a twofold problem for the teacher of writing. First, the teacher must be concerned with meeting the needs of diverse individuals and groups of students. Members of different ethnic, racial, and economic groups daily come together in the urban classroom, and in spite of homogeneous grouping, writing abilities vary widely among students. The scope of that variation, and thus the need for individualized instruction, have increased with the mainstreaming of handicapped students. Second, teachers must provide common learning experiences for students. The socializing function of schooling makes that demand and so do constraints arising from class sizes and time schedules.

I have found that the two sides of the problem, how to meet diverse needs and how to achieve uniformity, are not necessarily incompatible nor competing. Given the right strategies, the urban secondary composition teacher can meet differing student needs and still provide common learning experiences. It is not only possible, but also advisable. None of us likes to be often singled out for anything other than praise; for our students, too, becoming the object of too much uninvited individual attention can be discomforting in a group setting. Indeed, one main assumption behind both mainstreaming and desegregation is that both students and society benefit when school experiences are shared. Strategies that permit individualized instruction within a framework of shared and consistent activity, thus, are important for the teaching of writing in the urban classroom.

One such strategy that has worked very well for me is what I call class-mating. That label refers to the first essential component of the strategy, the matching or pairing of secondary classes with elementary ones. Class-mating provides a framework of shared and consistent activity. The objective is to practice writing for a particular audience, and even the most reluctant and unskilled writers in grades seven through twelve find elementary school students a natural and inviting

18

audience for their writing. The assignment that has worked best with the class-mating strategy for me is "Write a Children's Story."

If there is a secret to the success of class-mating, then it must be as simple as this: Younger children are a demanding audience, but not a threatening one. Writing has to be clear and error-free, informative and entertaining, to be acceptable to children, and those characteristics are not always easy for secondary school writers to achieve. Still, there is something about writing for younger children, perhaps the simple fact that the audience is younger, that makes the strategy work, even with secondary students for whom the development of writing skills presents seemingly insurmountable difficulties. I have tried the strategy with learning disabled students, with Spanish students, and with speakers of nonstandard dialects, and without exception the strategy has encouraged them to produce quality writing.

Class-mating provides a framework for shared activity in that students all do the same writing assignment for the same audience. Within that framework, writing workshop methods permit me to work with individual writers. In a given urban composition classroom there are writers who ask for a lot of teacher assistance, other writers who want very little help, and writers at every point between those extremes. Workshop methods, described later in this paper, permit teachers to meet those individual needs and demands.

The class-mating strategy, then, has two essential ingredients. Secondary school writers write for elementary school readers, and the teacher of writing works with individual writers. Those ingredients come together on one important aspect of the strategy: Every writer succeeds with the class-mating strategy. The writer's success, and the good feelings that go along with it, stem from the realization that, for this assignment at least, grades are less important than the impact of writing on an audience and that writing does not get published until that impact is assured.

The first step in implementing the class-mating strategy is to obtain permission from elementary teachers to match your secondary classes with theirs. Working through the school principal, explain that you would like your students to write children's stories for an audience of real children who will respond to the stories. Explain, also, that you would like several elementary grade classes to participate in the project, permitting your students to choose the grade level for which they will write. Principals and teachers have invariably welcomed the project with enthusiasm and agreed to distribute or read the stories to students and to help them respond to the stories. That response is written down, sometimes by the teacher and sometimes by the elementary students themselves, and is returned to my students.

Once permission from cooperating teachers has been obtained, introduce the project to your classes. Tell students that they will be writing stories for children, and that the stories will be read by children. Explain that each class has been matched with an elementary class and that children expect the stories to be delivered by a certain date. Allow at least one month for that deadline, so that even the slowest writers have time to write, revise, and edit their stories. Stress that success with this project will be determined by what the elementary school students say about the stories. That point is crucial. If other students are to serve as an audience for student writing, then the power of evaluation should belong to those students. More than anything else, the power of evaluation makes an audience real to a writer.

With the class-mating strategy, then, you stop being a teacher who instructs, reads, and grades students' writing. Instead, you become a consultant to individual writers, a partner or advisor who helps them get their stories ready for publication.

Using workshop methods allows all students to work through the assignment, but each at his or her own pace. The product in each case will be the same—a story ready to publish for a real, live audience. The process, though, will vary greatly and according to individual needs. To ensure that I meet those needs, I avoid talking to the whole class at once, and I insist that all of the writing for this project be done in class. In that manner, I can work with individual writers as writing problems arise.

Because students work through the class-mating assignments at individual rates, it is necessary to have additional work ready for students who complete the assignment before others. Two kinds of work have proven to be especially profitable: first, helping other writers, and second, doing another assignment for another audience. Either option makes more sense than busy work such as that found in vocabulary or sentence combining workbooks, because writing or helping others to write is more meaningful and maintains the framework of shared and consistent activity.

I have witnessed a number of widely varying individual needs. Some students need to do research before they write. That research often consists of reading one or two children's stories to get a feel for the genre. Other students need to get a feel for the audience, and conversations with others who have young brothers or sisters help them get started. Many students need to be reminded that anything is possible in children's stories. Encourage reluctant writers to trust their imaginations—for example, to make rabbits talk or robots fly. For others, imagination is not the answer; encourage them to write factually, as in writing advice on how to make or do something, since writing a story is not as important as writing. One student, for example, rewrote an autobiography of Frederick Douglass for younger children. For students whose writing problems are severe, I encourage the one-sentence-per-page type of story.

One major advantage of the class-mating strategy is that students of English as a second language and speakers of nonstandard dialects begin to understand the necessity of using standard English for published writing. Given the writing workshop structure, I have been able to build on that understanding, for example, by helping Spanish-speaking students with the past tense of regular English verbs, or by helping speakers of the black English vernacular eliminate one nonstandard form at a time from their writing, such as the deletion of the final *s* for plural formation.

The class-mating strategy has much to recommend it. Writing for a real audience beats studying how to reach audiences or writing for imagined audiences. Because writing is published, the strategy teaches student writers the significance of absolutely clean, error-free copy. More importantly, the strategy provides time and opportunities for teachers to help students, according to each one's individual needs, while every member of the class works toward the same objective.

Dealing with Differences
by Accentuating Them?

Jack Folsom
Montana State University

In any English classroom containing twenty-five or more students, there is high probability that all of the "different" groups will be represented: the physically handicapped, the speaker of non-native or nonstandard language, the gifted and talented, the nontraditional. One can assume that most or all of these students, to the extent that they are aware of their differences, would just as soon not have attention drawn to them. Most of these students have already received cruel treatment from at least some of their peers and teachers, and their self-esteem may be correspondingly diminished. Having been one of these students myself, I can understand why others would want to remain as closed-up and anonymous as possible. Anyone who is "different" in the adolescent subculture is a despicable freak.

The irony in this situation lies in the fact that, despite the sameness of the majority, *all* students are different in some ways. These differences, if rightly seen and acknowledged by a class community, can be a source of great interest to a class and of great pride for the individual whose differences are displayed among those of others. As one of my students wrote, in the midst of the project I am going to describe, "uniqueness is a universal characteristic that allows each individual a pride in his history." That student was too naive to say his or *her* history, but she herself was already swelling with pride at the thought of the word *history* being used in reference to her short life.

The project is entitled, "I am the only person here who _____." I began it by explaining to the class that with all of the leveling forces that we are experiencing nowadays, many of us feel less like people and more like numbers. Even the presence of the students in this class has been determined by a computer, and anyone who seems to be colored green or to have six fingers on one hand is bound to get hassled by someone. I then said that I was going to make some bets with the class, and that they were going to make some bets with each other: I was going to bet that I was the only person here who _____, and I listed five items on the board. I was careful to list things which were not impossible for them; therefore, I told them that I was leaving out the fact that I have been married for twenty-six years, a sure winner on the betting. So I listed other items: that I was born in Connecticut (good winning chance for a class in Montana), that I have a crooked nose (poor chance, and I lost), that I have skied the Olympic courses in Innsbruck, Austria (good chance to win, but I lost), that I wear eyeglasses with clear plastic frames (a winner when one of the students added that they looked "wimpy"), and finally, my principal difference, that as a child I was bedridden for two years with nephrosis, a kidney disease that had 85 percent mortality at the time (I bet on that one confidently).

Now that the students had become somewhat interested in my differences (self-disclosure by teachers does humanize them, after all, in the eyes of students), I transferred the students' interest to themselves and each other. They were to list five items: five things from your life history or things about you which most likely distinguish you from anyone else here. After listing them they shared them with a partner or small group, questioning each other on the experience or on what it is like to be colored green or to have six toes. The homework was an exercise in pattern recognition and synthesis: Write a single paragraph containing the five items, controlled by a main idea. What they realized when they attempted the paragraph is that what they had listed in the first place were probably things that they were in some way proud of, even if the item had been depressing at the time or disastrous.

The paragraphs often turned out to be narratives-in-brief, surrounding the sentences containing each item. Many students felt inclined to make interpretive comment; others simply listed in sentence form, then stood back and declared, "These things in my past have indeed been unique, and I look forward to those of the future."

The next steps in the project are fairly obvious: After discussion of your paragraph with the partner or small group, expand each item into a paragraph of its own, supplying more details and opinions of the feature or experience. Then in class, brainstorm connections and ordering of the paragraphs into a mini-autobiography. This can in turn become part of a class anthology of uniqueness, in which all can take pride.

Here are some examples of what I got:

1. A girl who is one-quarter Chippewa-Cree Indian, the wandering tribe. Knowing that some of her relatives had migrated north to Canada, she herself went hiking in the Northwest Territories.

2. A boy who recalled how his father, a veterinarian, removed a

face-full of porcupine quills from the family Labrador—unlikely to be a unique experience in rural America, but one which somehow enriched the life of the writer.

3. A girl who saw challenge in all of her items: uprooting from home and moving to a new state, learning the French language, living in Norway as an exchange student, nearly drowning while water-skiing.

4. A girls whose items all reflected the suffering she had witnessed: her grandfather's death, an entire city destroyed by fire— experiences which led her to conclude: "I have found it is through something bad that something good is born."

5. A boy who became fascinated by the past, especially by the cultures and languages of the Crow and Blackfeet tribes. He bet that he was the only one in the class who had made a *capote*, a heavy coat worn by hunters and trappers that is made from Hudson's Bay blankets.

6. A girl who concluded that she was "a rare breed": Coming from a very ethnic Italian family with some Cherokee ancestry, she declared, must have brought out in her the love of living dangerously, and she listed some items.

Where are the handicapped, the non-native speakers, the gifted and talented, the nonstandard speakers, or the nontraditional students in these examples? As it happens, I had no non-native speakers in that class, but every other "different" group was represented. That they made no issue of "that sort" of difference is not surprising. The most noticeably different student, unmistakably a Native American Indian, discussed matter-of-factly and proudly her experience with beadwork and the playing of woodwind instruments, as if she were saying, "Know me in my uniqueness, and know me as just like you."

There were at least two gifted and talented students in the class. Both carefully avoided mention of the fact, but they showed it in the wit and ingenuity of their writing. There was one student who was handicapped: He was almost paralyzed by shyness, keeping his head down most of the time. He turned in nothing for the assignment, but later he wrote a creditable paper on procrastination and felt comfortable enough with me for what I had done to seek an individual conference for help on another assignment. Without the "I bet I am the only person here who _____" project, that student would be in the "loss" column of my records today.

A classroom project like the one I have described would seem to be valuable in building the confidence and motivation of students who are different, but there are inherent dangers involved. Often in the past, teachers have either pretended to ignore the differences of handicapped, minority, disadvantaged, or otherwise nontraditional students in their classrooms, or else they have drawn undue attention to these differences. I know of one student who looks retarded but isn't, who has courageously continued her education in her motorized wheelchair, and who repeatedly encounters well-meaning teachers and students who want to make an issue of her handicap and her efforts to surmount it. This student finally had to drop one class because, as she said, "I was constantly being put under a microscope." She kept smiling as it happened, but she cried at home.

The idea in a project like mine is not to draw attention to the difference that the student is self-conscious about (unless that student wants that to happen), but to the differences that the student feels are somehow unique and potentially interesting to others, so that the student can join the classroom community and feel welcome. Those special, individualized requirements related to the "special" difference should be managed one-on-one outside the classroom. The principle is to raise the issue of differences with a class, but to substitute what one can take pride in for what makes one feel demeaned or embarrassed.

"Know me in my uniqueness, and know me as just like you."

Failure Is No Fun:
A Competency-Based Approach
That Generates Success

Mort Sherman, Ray Betti, Doris Chiappetta, and Marcia Supon
Coleytown Junior High School, Westport, Connecticut

With the all too familiar cry, "They're lacking some basic skills," ringing in our ears, we began another year trying to teach "modified" classes. Difficult, outmoded books and "busy work" ditto sheets abounded—so did anxiety and frustration. Underlying it all, however, was the noticeable love, respect, and understanding we shared for each other. Our students knew we cared. We mirrored each other's frustrations. Once we, as teachers, began to share our thoughts and feelings, the floodgates opened. In a myriad of ways our students expressed their need to succeed. They wanted to be like the "regular" students. They wanted to be smart and to enjoy learning. No one wanted to come to school just to meet failure; however, that's what they saw and felt after years of reinforced failure. We knew we had to begin by modifying attitudes—theirs and ours.

The first step was to allow each student to let off steam. Once or twice a week, anyone could call for a rap session. Most importantly, we shared our feelings—likes, dislikes, problems, failures, and anger. We teachers shared too. Our sharings enabled students to know that at times we were not pleased with our actions or self-images. Students began to realize that, like them, we had difficulty accepting rejection. From these sessions grew the realization that all of us are vulnerable. This, of course, was the problem that seemed to permeate the sessions. The students wanted to be part of the whole, even though they saw themselves as different because of physical handicaps and/or their previous inability to succeed academically.

Success meant more than the clichés "You're as good as anyone," or "You can do it, if you try." They *knew* they couldn't do *some* things, no matter how much effort was exerted. In some instances, the students were more realistic about their limitations than we. They were bitter. They needed to believe and feel rather than know that we sincerely loved them. They had to be shown—a touch on the arm as we walked up and down the aisles, a wink or a smile in the halls or in the cafeteria developed a bond among us. The bond became stronger and stronger and the attitudes toward one another began to change.

Disciplining with love was our guide. Armed with a strong desire to create a positive change, we knew we could affect behavior. If we could reaffirm good behavior with a smile, a touch, or a wink, we could discipline with that same love. A stern directive to apologize for rude behavior, or a frown when someone dumped someone else's books, soon began to take effect. Killer statements (put downs) had to go.

Everything seemed to click at the same time. We knew in September that the traditional teaching approach was not working. As we opened to one another and as we became more sensitive to the needs of our students, we developed a new program—a specialized curriculum for our "special" people.

The Population

Coleytown Junior High School in Westport, Connecticut, which houses grades six through nine, has several curricular approaches. The sixth grade operates on a cluster or team approach, using the facilities of the building yet remaining on a different schedule. The seventh through ninth grades operate on a traditional departmental approach. Main-streamed into each grade level are some students from the Coleytown Developmental Center (C.D.C.). C.D.C., a regional program for children with special needs, functions as a school-within-a-school.

In addition to the students from C.D.C., not all of whom are main-streamed, many students in the regular program are in need of special attention. To meet these needs, the English department has created two levels of courses in the seventh grade. The "modified" level (no more than fifteen students per class) is designed to meet the needs of those students identified as needing extra help. The "regular" level is for students who can perform without the aid of a modified program. The eighth and ninth grades add a third level. This level, an honors section, is for students who have demonstrated a high level of proficiency in the language arts.

The Program

The modified program is one which is designed to provide as much individual instruction as possible in a classroom setting. Students are placed in a modified class for a plethora of reasons: disciplinary problems, learning disability, physical handicap, or emotional adjustment.

Clearly, the problem is how to deal with such a varied group of students who acutely need individual attention.

The previous modified program allowed teachers to be autonomous, to be creative, and to deal with the students as best they could. Using worksheets, oral reading, magazines, and adolescent literature, the previous program dealt with students on a stopgap basis. Similar to many other programs, our modified program was not felt to meet the needs of the students.

Rather than give lip service to the ideal of individual instruction, those of us involved with the program set out to develop a curriculum which did not teach whole lessons to whole classes. Central to our concerns was how to present a program wherein students of varied capabilities and interests could succeed and yet be taught necessary skills. Concentrating on the affective, the new program has met with tremendous success.

The heart of the program is love, understanding, and honesty blended with and balanced against responsibility, limitations, and realistic expectations. As a staff we share these feelings; our students, although not always able or anxious to vocalize, share them, too.

In order to better address the needs of our students, we teamed into units of one male and one female. These teams proved to be a wise division because some students respond and relate to one sex model more positively than to the other. This division in teaming is vital at this age level generally, and with problem students specifically.

The program we developed is competency-based. With a blending of teacher-directed activities with independent student choice, the units are thematic and vary in both scope and sequence. The exercises are divided into three levels of difficulty, each exercise offering the opportunity to try a different level. The final grade is based upon the number of exercises completed, not upon the difficulty of each one. To assure continuity and consistency of the academic program, certain exercises must be completed by all students. Even within this structure, however, the program is totally adaptable so that physically and emotionally handicapped students can find success. The list below demonstrates some adaptations which may be used with different student handicaps.

Handicap	*Adaptation*
Quadriplegic with gross motor control of arms and hands	1. Set a time limit for written work rather than requiring a certain amount of writing.

	2.	Have the student do some work orally or use a tape recorder in place of the written work.
Hearing impaired	1.	Seat the student in the center front of the class.
	2.	Make sure the teacher never stands and talks with the student when the teacher's back is to the window.
	3.	Use language experience.
	4.	Evaluate the concept or idea, not the sophistication of its presentation.
Emotionally disturbed	1.	Begin with the affective domain.
	2.	Quickly focus the student on an exercise where immediate (within the period) success is achieved.
Learning disabled	1.	Encourage the use of different levels where success is all but guaranteed (level 3 spelling, level 1 plot line, for example).
	2.	Depending upon the disability, modify quantity of written work, presentation of ideas (art, music), and/or amount of teacher-vs.-student structuring of the unit.

To begin a unit, students and teachers read, discuss, and clarify the material which will be used as the basis of the unit. After this teacher-directed introduction, the students proceed to work on the exercises of their choice. Each unit is structured so that the basic cognitive components of the language arts are covered. The chart below details exercises which form a unit based on "The Cask of Amontillado" by Poe.

Cognitive Process	Skill Area	Specific Exercise
Listening	Audiovisual	Listen to another story (record) and discuss it
Speaking	Explaining, defending, presenting	Student-teacher, student-student dialogues

	Oral reading	Fluency and rate, expression
Writing	Comprehension	*Literal:* sentence writing using vocabulary *Inferential:* put the narrator in a different setting (our school) and have him respond to a situation "in character"
Reading	Comprehension	*Literal:* plot line, short answer, cloze, spelling, vocabulary, dictionary work *Inferential:* descriptive phrases of narrator, of Fortunato

Learning Stations

Fifteen learning stations were offered in the "Cask of Amontillado" unit. The students were free to choose among the fifteen, though seven stations, which dealt with the most basic areas, were required. The chart that follows is a copy of the evaluation sheet used by each student. The chart lists the fifteen stations with space for notes concerning date of completion, level of difficulty, and teacher's initials.

Students are given new folders at the beginning of each unit. This helps set the tone that each unit is a new beginning. In each folder is stored the evaluation sheet for the unit and, if necessary, a copy of the story. Starred units must be completed first; however, they may be completed in any order. All work is stored in each student's folder. As a general rule, folders do not go home. Depending upon the child, we try to set some kind of time limit for the completion of certain exercises before we request that an exercise be finished as homework.

Along with the freedom to choose their own work for any given day, the students are given the opportunity to choose the level of difficulty on which to work. Each station has three levels. Level I is most difficult, Level II is less difficult, and Level III is easiest.

Although there is no grade reward or penalty for working on difficult or easy levels, most students choose the more challenging levels. The students want to prove to us, to their peers, and to themselves that they can do challenging work. We rarely have to suggest that a student work on a higher level. In fact, we find that more often we tactfully have to suggest that a student work on an easier level.

Teacher's Initials	Level	Date		
			*Spelling	
			*Locate word	Vocabulary
			*Look up in dictionary	Vocabulary
			*Write sentence	Vocabulary
			Extra credit Flash cards	Vocabulary
			Figures of speech	Comprehension
			*Descriptive phrases	Comprehension
			*Audiovisual	Comprehension
			*Phrases/ narrator	Structure
			Plot line	Structure
			*Three-sentence character sketch	Composition
			Cloze	Evaluation
			Sentence out of context	Evaluation
			Short answer	Evaluation
			Bulletin board extra credit	Evaluation

"The Cask of Amontillado" by Edgar Allan Poe

Your Name: _____

The spelling unit provides a good example to illustrate the three levels. In order to master the spelling station on Level I, a student must learn the correct spelling of 20 words; for Level II, 15 words; and, for Level III, 10 words.

Grading System

One of the most successful and encouraging aspects of the program is the removal of the "mystery" from grades for these students. Grades had become threatening; they seemed arbitrary, and often seemed to be a punishment rather than a reward. In order to have a truly success-oriented program, students must feel as if they are capable.

In the "Cask of Amontillado" unit, students are required to complete a minimum of seven stations to obtain a grade of C. Their grades increase in proportion to the number of stations mastered. The students receive credit for the station when it is successfully completed on any of the three levels. Students become very excited when they realize how "easy" it is to get a good grade.

This marking system has had some extraordinary and unexpected results. When, perhaps for the first time, students realize that they are in control of their grades, some begin to ask if they can "please" take some work home. Others ask if they can bring their folders to study hall to do extra work to improve their grades. Before this program was adopted, these requests were simply unthinkable.

In conclusion, the students and the teachers involved with this program are convinced that it works. The reasons for this success are several. First, this program is planned by the teachers who use it; thus, the teachers' acceptance of the program and their understanding of the students is assured. Second, the students are afforded every possible opportunity for success. Third, administrative support for all aspects of the program is an encouraging reality.

2 Students Facing Obstacles to Learning

Dealing with Visual Impairment in the English Classroom

Beverly A. McColley
Brandon Junior High School, Virginia Beach, Virginia

When I first learned that I would have a visually impaired student in my remedial English class, I felt sorry for myself. I thought of all the transparencies I had prepared, wondering how I would cope with his inability to see anything projected on the overhead. I worried about the many changes I would have to make to accommodate his handicap.

Fortunately, sometime between my initial reaction and Frank's arrival, my attitude changed. Helping Frank adjust to the class became a challenge instead of a burden. Even before the students reported to class, I assigned preferential seating to Frank. This meant he did not have to suffer the embarrassment of being moved to the front. The itinerant teacher assigned to facilitate mainstreaming provided many valuable aids. She even furnished SRA tests with large print and was present to give Frank special help during the administration of the test. She also provided a yellow-tinted transparency which gives greater contrast and legibility when placed over dittos. On reading days Frank can listen to stories on tape, using a tape recorder and headphones which she provided. He also has an assortment of special magnifying lenses that enable him to read books as well as see the board. Other students in the class have not been distracted by these aids but have accepted them as part of the classroom routine.

An unexpected result has been the fact that innovations made to help Frank in particular have been a benefit to the whole class. Students in this eighth-grade remedial class range from third to fifth grade in reading level. I started reading the questions on tests mainly to help Frank but noticed that scores improved for the whole class. They knew the answers but sometimes had difficulty reading the questions. I have also made frequent use of taped stories in order to help Frank. The whole class, however, enjoys the activity of following the text while listening to a taped, dramatic reading of the material. The use of a combined visual and auditory approach seems to improve the comprehension and vocabulary of slow readers. In order to eliminate having the student take lengthy class notes or copy homework assignments—a tedious task for Frank—I began typing dittos of all homework assignments, with an explanation at the top. In the past, remedial students were always hostile (understandably) when given assignments to copy. Now they are free to concentrate on the skills being taught rather than spend class time in copying. This procedure has also reduced my need for the overhead. However, when I must use the overhead, I allay Frank's fear by reading the material slowly. He also knows that when I am finished, I will remove the transparency and pass it to him for examination.

The most rewarding part of these efforts has been the natural adjustment Frank has made to the class. Lately he has been writing mysteries in his journal and has asked to share them with the class. The students listen intently and with enjoyment as Frank, nose pressed to his journal, shares with the class his most recent creative writing. He reads slowly but with good projection and obvious delight.

Frank's adjustment to the class and his discovery that writing can be fun have made him an asset instead of a liability. Instead of inhibiting my teaching as I had feared, having a visually impaired student in my class has improved both my techniques and rewards as a teacher.

Children's Literature to See and Hear: A Total Communication Approach

Barbara Dreher
Wright State University

Ellen Duell
Dayton, Ohio, City Schools

A total communication approach to children's literature is the simultaneous visual presentation and signed interpretation of books on split screen television. Total communication is the method for teaching language to the deaf and to some mentally retarded or aphasic children. It is currently popular because it combines both lip-reading and sign language. It supplements oral/aural hearing aid instruction with signs and finger spelling to give as many cues as possible to the handicapped child. This approach to well-chosen books enhances the possibility that such children will grow in artistic and literary appreciation along with their age mates.

Need and Purposes

Deaf or hearing impaired children are generally two grades behind in reading (Kretschmer, et al., 1978). The need for building a language system without natural auditory input keeps them from enjoying with age peers the usual language arts activities in a mainstreamed classroom. Literature, the raw material for teaching humanistic values, cannot be appreciated at the proper time if the child has to read it alone. The deaf child at ten may just have achieved the ability to read the large picture books seen in the kindergarten, but their content and themes are no longer of interest.

Through videotaping simultaneously the illustrations and a signed interpretation of the text, auditory and reading problems are circumvented. Deaf, aphasic, or mentally retarded children who receive instruction in sign, will have a chance to appreciate literature appropriate to their mental maturity. Children without handicaps can enjoy the vocal narration and sound effects. They may glean a secondary benefit from observation of the order and beauty of signed communication.

The goals for such a project are to provide opportunities for deaf and hearing children to experience books of literary and artistic quality; to teach and confirm children's growth in understanding and sensory awareness; to enrich cognitive growth through the primary experiences of the videotapes, and through follow-up activities designed to increase cognitive skills on ascending levels; to enrich affective development through identification with characters and feelings expressed in the selections, and through follow-up activities including discussion, interpretive movement, pantomime, creative dramatics or role play, self-expression through language and graphic arts.

Principles and Problems in Book Selection

Books should be chosen for literary and artistic excellence, for intellectual integrity, and for their presentation of human values. Children of both sexes and all races should be able to identify with the characters and experiences portrayed. Any books chosen for informational value should be accurate in both text and illustrations. In the above respects, choosing a book for signed videotaping is no different than choosing a book for reading aloud to a classroom of normal children.

For this project there were additional criteria. The visual component of the book should be strong enough to suit effective videotaping. Large, bold, colorful illustrations will carry best. Pictures with fairly heavy, black outlining will look almost three-dimensional on screen. Illustrations with thin lines, fine details, and lack of vibrancy will not carry well. Print on the illustration page should be avoided. Children who are absorbed in watching the hands, face, and lips of the interpreter do not need a reading lesson at the same time.

Complex pictures should be avoided because they have too much "noise." When children are inundated with more visual information than they can assimilate they become confused. What they see in a picture is determined by their background knowledge and perceptual set. The more irrelevant data in an illustration, the more ways it can be interpreted and the greater chances for distraction. Books that afford the greatest correspondence between words and pictures will be the most helpful for language comprehension and learning with this special population.

This fact brings us to a real caution. How much can a hearing impaired or retarded child attend to at one time? At what speed? While a hearing adult may complain that picture books are static and the videotape moves slowly, the message is probably not being received solely through sign. The listener hears the narrator and fails to take in all of the movement and action on the interpreter's side of the screen. The picture side of the screen will have whatever activity the plot and techniques, such as zooming and panning, will allow. Speed and surprise views are not desired if literary goals are to be achieved by communicatively handicapped children.

Finally, books are chosen to promote humanistic values and to alleviate the emotional and personal problems most children face. In developing greater self-knowledge through the literary mechanisms of identification, compensation, and rationalization, the youngster develops empathy for other people. Vicarious experiences expand the ego-centric thinking Piaget has described for this age group to allow for role taking. Appropriate books give social and emotional insights. They help children cope with the fears of childhood, sibling rivalry, physical differences, separation, frustration, low self-esteem, and other sources of personal unease (Rubin, 1979).

Preparing Scripts

Visually—Two video cameras and two copies of the book will be necessary to avoid breaks for page turning. The director cannot assume that the pages can be turned in order. By careful study of the text the camera can be directed to the objects or actions mentioned first. Any print on a page with a picture should be covered over. It is not only unpleasant visually, but it is distracting and adds to visual "noise." Movement can be introduced by panning the scene or zooming in or away from details in the picture.

Literally—When narration is done with different voices, identifying phrases ("said the painter") should be deleted from the text. Some of the words may have to be replaced by simpler equivalents ("overjoyed" = "very happy"; "refused" = "said no") because they don't suit either the cognitive level of the child or the signing system.

Videotaping

A minimum of three cameras is needed—two for the illustrations and one for the signer. To avoid the necessity of using cue cards or having the interpreter memorize the text, an off-camera narrator reads the script. The signer, then, has audio cues for the message being mouthed or whispered (sotto voce) and signed. Two microphones are needed if the narrator is assisted by other actors doing any other voices the script requires. Music and sound effects are dubbed in to make the finished product palatable and aesthetically complete.

Implementation

In fantasy, a child witnesses what he or she can't experience literally and, in the comparison between the imaginary world and the actual world, finds validity in the emotions portrayed in the former. This fact led us to the choice of a fantasy for the first videotaped book.

Feeling lonely or separate is common to all children in some situations. It is not the hallmark of the handicapped. A possible remedy is in a song from the famous musical, *The Sound of Music:* "When the bee stings, when the dog bites, when I'm feeling sad, I simply remember my favorite things and then I don't feel so bad."

Loneliness, however, does not preclude the possibility of joyful rejoining and love. Exploration of such feelings was an ultimate goal of the total communication presentation of Max Velthuijs' book, *The Painter and the Bird.* It is a fantasy about an artist who sells his favorite picture, that of a "strange and wonderful" bird. But the bird flies out of the picture and out of the rich buyer's mansion, to find his true friend, the painter. After several misadventures the two are happily reunited. Here is the study guide for the previewing and postviewing discussion and activities.

Study Guide

The Painter and the Bird, by Max Velthuijs

   A. Previewing discussion
      1. Do you have a favorite teddy bear or toy, picture or book?
        a. Would you sell it to someone else?
        b. Suppose you were offered a lot of money for it?
        c. Would you feel lonely without it?
      2. What is a "painter"? (Several answers are acceptable. Elicit the information that this painter paints pictures to sell for money to buy his food, clothes, and home.)
   B. Postviewing discussion
      1. Was the painter rich?
      2. Was he happy?
      3. What did he love? Which was his *favorite* picture?
      4. Who came to look at the paintings?
      5. Why did the painter finally decide to sell the picture of the strange and wonderful bird to the rich man?
      6. How did the painter feel when the rich man walked away

with the picture? Do you remember the look on the painter's face as the rich man left?

7. Where did the rich man take the painting?
8. How did the strange and wonderful bird feel in the rich man's house? Why?
9. What did the bird do then?
10. Could a painted bird really have sad feelings, as a living bird can? Could it actually fly out of the picture? How do you know?
11. Did you like to think that the bird missed the painter? What makes it all right to make believe or pretend something? (Knowing the difference.)
12. What did the bird do next?
13. Would it have been just as good a story if there had been no make-believe? How then could the painter have gotten his bird picture back?

C. Activities
1. Paint or draw a bird, animal, or object to put up in your room and keep you company.
2. Write a short story or poem about your favorite things.
3. What are your mother's favorite things? Your dad's? Your friend's?
4. Learn the song "My Favorite Things" from *The Sound of Music.* (Deaf children can learn it as a poem, and may use percussion beats for rhythmic accompaniment.
5. Walk as though you are sad, missing your favorite thing or person. Now walk as you would when it returns to you.

References

Kretschmer, R., Kretschmer, L., and Strong, R. *Language Learning and Deafness.* New York: Grune and Stratton, 1978.

Rubin, J. R., *Using Bibliotherapy.* Berkeley, Calif.: Oryx Press/ Neal-Schuman Associates, 1979.

Using Chapters: Reading and Writing at Different Levels

James M. Deem
Mohawk Valley Community College, Utica, New York

Sandra A. Engel
Mohawk Valley Community College, Utica, New York

The college students enrolled in our integrated reading and basic writing course have been placed there on the basis of their scores on a standardized reading test and a holistically scored writing sample. In reading, they have scored below the fourth stanine; in writing, they have scored below college entry level. Often, however, their low scores and their histories of failure seem to be all these students have in common, for their actual abilities vary greatly: Some students read word for word with no word attack skills, while others comprehend fairly well yet read at a painstaking rate. Similarly, in writing, some students are unable to match their speech to writing, while others need instruction in developing sentences or ideas.

Such a mixture of students is difficult to fit into a traditional instructional format. On the one hand, individualization seems to be the answer. However, many of these students have such low self-esteem and have had such limited involvement in their secondary classrooms that group instruction also seems both valuable and necessary.

One way we have discovered of balancing the individual with the group is a technique we call "chapter reading," based on an idea presented in Smith (1979). Chapter reading enables us to deal with the individual abilities of our students while at the same time allowing us to develop a sense of community. This sense of group cohesiveness in turn results in a real audience for the students' writing and a real interest in and reason for reading.

Smith's suggestion was intended to increase the motivation of young children for reading. A novel was to be divided into chapters or sections so that each student could read and share one part of the story. This, in turn, would motivate the students to read more and develop better attitudes toward reading. Smith, however, warns against formalizing the activity, because its rewarding aspects could then be viewed as punitive —a problem with young, reluctant readers. Our version of Smith's approach incorporates more structure, since older students are involved, yet we have not overlooked the motivational aspects of Smith's approach.

One book we have used for chapter reading is *Compromising Positions,* an adult murder mystery. Excluding the final chapter, we divided the book into fifteen sections, one for each of our fifteen students. Some students received one chapter, others received two, with section lengths ranging from 12 to 40 pages. We then assigned these to different students based on the students' initial reading test scores. Generally speaking, the poorest readers received the shortest chapters, although one relatively short chapter was assigned to a better reader because of its fairly technical discussion of Don Juanism.

Before we handed out the chapters to the students, an annotated character list, a summary, and study questions for each student had to be prepared. The character list was the easiest to prepare since the same list could be provided for each student. The summaries were another matter, however. Since every student brought a different reading ability to the book and since every student began the book in a different place, summaries were tailored for each student.

For the poorer readers the summaries provided more detail than for the better readers, with more explanations to make certain events clear. Very little was taken for granted in the poorer readers' summaries. Better readers received the main events with less explanation. Summarizing any mystery, with the convolutions of plot, is a feat, but writing fourteen cumulative summaries (since one was not needed for the person with Chapter One), though difficult, was not impossible. Finally, study questions were written for each section. Again the questions were tailored for each student. Poorer readers were sometimes given page numbers to aid them in answering questions, while better readers were often asked more inferential questions.

Prior to handing out the chapters and supplementary materials, we prepared the students for the reading. Students transcribed a dictation (part of our attempt to teach oral/written correspondence) which discussed the book. A day beforehand, we explained the assignment and asked students to attend the following day, since the assignment depended on the cooperation of fifteen students.

On the assignment day, a Friday, each student was present. Each received the list of characters, a summary, study questions, and the chapter itself. As further stimulus to read the book, we gave a presentation of the cover and pre-title page.

The students were instructed to familiarize themselves with the character list, to read the summary, to read their sections, and to answer the study questions by Monday. On Monday we planned to cover the vocabulary they had found to be difficult in their reading; then they would have another night to reread their sections before they prepared a written summary of their sections in class.

On Monday we fielded words from the class, wrote them on the board, and gave an informal definition of each. The words some students found difficult (e.g., *occasionally*) other students found to be very easy, but all students were invited to learn new vocabulary from their sections.

Tuesday, after rereading their sections, students were instructed to write a summary of their section, to share with the other students in class the following day. The summaries were to cover the murder, the narrator's involvement in the investigation, and the narrator's dissolving marriage. Other information was to be considered less important unless a study question probed for other information. Both of the instructors worked individually with the students, helping them focus on the important parts of their sections, a task some of the poorer writers found particularly difficult. While most had a good idea of the main events from reading their sections, they had difficulty expressing the main ideas in writing. Consequently, the kind of wine that two characters shared over lunch might be included in a student's first draft without the benefit of the instructor's guidance. However, since the students knew that they were writing for their classmates, they were motivated to produce their best writing. As a result, some who needed additional help from the writing lab tutor sought it in order to complete their summaries.

Wednesday, the students began to share their sections either by reading their summary or simply telling their information. Confusing parts were clarified with the class's help, and most of the book was covered. At the end of the hour, we handed out a copy of the last chapter to each student which we asked them to read for the following day. We told them that the murderer's identity and motive were given in the chapter, but we did not supply a summary or study questions.

Thursday, we concluded the remaining sections and as a group discussed the last chapter. Everyone had taken the time to read it; everyone was intrigued with discovering the murderer's identity. After we completed the discussion, a number of students asked, "Can we do this again?"

We certainly do plan to continue this activity. At this point we have taught four novels for chapter reading in the course of a year. All are mysteries and while none can be classified as literature, the students have enjoyed reading and writing about them. We have found that a mystery seems to work best with the chapter reading approach, in that there is more incentive to unravel the plot and predict the ending.

Chapter reading as we have described it can be a valuable instructional activity for instructors who have enough time to design such an activity. However, the rewards seem to offset the time involved: Some of these fifteen students, who had never read an entire book, "finished" the entire book in a matter of days and made a valuable contribution to the group. They became interested in reading and had a reason for their writing. They had even found it all enjoyable, a word they had not previously associated with such activities. Although the students' abilities varied, their reactions to chapter reading did not.

Chapter reading is only one approach to the teaching of reading and basic writing. We have found it an activity the provides for both individual and group activities. Perhaps most importantly, we have found it valuable in motivating students to write not only summaries, but their own stories; to read not only chapters, but entire books.

Reference

Smith, Cyrus F., Jr. " 'Read a Book in an Hour': Variations to Develop Composition and Comprehension Skills." *Journal of Reading*, 23, *1* (October 1979), pp. 25–29.

Wordless Picture Books and the Learning Disabled

Karen D'Angelo
State University of New York–Binghamton

Success in reading for learning disabled children and youth can start with wordless picture books. In these textless books, stories can be inferred from the interrelated pictures. These picture books are being published in increasing numbers today and can be found on most library shelves. They vary in artistic style and story content from simple to intricate, but all share one valuable distinction—they contain no words.

In elementary schools, kindergarten and first grade children and their teachers are the primary users of picture books without words. These books are being used to stimulate reading readiness and oral language development in young children who cannot yet read or write (Degler, 1979; Huck, 1976; Larrick, 1976; Sutherland and Arbuthnot, 1977). Wordless picture books are also being used with young children and older students to develop a variety of writing skills (Abrahamson, 1977; D'Angelo, 1979).

Picture books which tell stories but have no text can also be explored with many learning disabled children in elementary classrooms. These books can be used with children who have not yet learned to read or may be having difficulty in reading printed materials. Wordless picture books can be used with the child who needs to develop skill in oral language, which is important in learning to read. With wordless books, the child who may or may not be able to read is not restricted by print which normally occurs in books. The child can invent dialog and narration as spoken words are supplied to accompany pictures and tell a story.

Four simple starter questions which can be used to initiate conversations about wordless picture books to help develop the child's descriptive and expressive speaking vocabularies are:

1. What things do you see in the picture?
2. What is happening in the picture?

3. What do you think will happen next?
4. Why do you think so?

New words can be added to the child's vocabulary as pictures are examined and colors, shapes, objects, animals, and people are named. A question which can begin this activity is "What things do you see in the picture?" All wordless books offer opportunities to develop vocabulary. Following are short reviews of a few books which serve this purpose especially well because of their content.

> *Anno's Alphabet* by Mitsumasa Anno contains pictures of woodblock letters and drawings of objects to go with each letter.
>
> *Noah's Ark* by Peter Spier tells the biblical story of Noah who loads the ark with all kinds of animals.
>
> *Count and See* by Tana Hoban contains photographs with counting from 1 to 15, by tens to 50, and ends with 100 peas in their pods.
>
> *Big Ones, Little Ones* by Tana Hoban contains color photographs of adult animals with their young.
>
> *Do You Want to Be My Friend?* by Eric Carle shows a mouse following the tails of one animal after another in pursuit of a friend.
>
> *Elephant Buttons* by Noriko Ueno shows an elephant's buttons popping open to reveal a lion, whose buttons pop to reveal a horse, and so on, down to a mouse.

Phrases and sentences which describe activity in pictures can be elicited from the child. A starter question which can help is "What is happening in the picture?" There are many wordless books which clearly show actions that can be explained and described in just a few words or in longer sentences. Descriptions of some are:

> *The Great Cat Chase* by John Goodall tells the story of children playing with a cat, dressed in doll clothes, that jumps out of a carriage and is pursued through a series of mishaps.
>
> *Changes, Changes* by Pat Hutchins shows two wooden dolls who arrange and rearrange blocks to deal with problems brought on by a fire and a flood.
>
> *Journey to the Moon* by Erich Fuchs tells the story of the Apollo 11 mission in photographs.
>
> *Out! Out! Out!* by Martha Alexander shows the chaos which develops when a bird enters the home of a little boy and adults try to capture it.

Looking at pictures and telling a story from beginning to end offers the child an opportunity to produce statements in logical order. Questions which can promote logical sequencing are "What is happening in the picture?" and "What do you think will happen next?" Many wordless books depict an ordered sequence of events and can be easily interpreted. Three such books are described as follows:

> *The Apple and the Moth* by Iela and Enzo Mari contains illustrations that follow a moth through egg, caterpillar, cocoon, and adult stages.

> *The Chicken and the Egg* by Iela and Enzo Mari shows an egg during the process of hatching.

> *Apples* by Nonny Hogrogian shows a parade of animals and people who carelessly toss apple cores away; eventually an apple orchard appears.

> *The Self-Made Snowman* by Fernando Krahn shows the progression of events beginning with snow rolling down a mountain and ending with creation of a snowman in the center of a town.

The child can also learn to predict actions, events, and feelings and express these ideas verbally. Skill in making predictions and confirming these guesses with evidence from the story involves comprehension that is basic to reading. Questions which serve this purpose and can be used with the following books are: "What do you think will happen next?" and "Why do you think so?"

> *Family* by Ellie Simmons tells the story of how a small girl deals with the arrival of a new baby in the family.

> *The Wrong Side of the Bed* by Edward Ardizzone realistically shows several incidents in the day of a little boy who gets out of bed, cross and scowling.

> *Frog Where Are You?* and *Frog Goes to Dinner* by Mercer Mayer contains three main characters: boy, dog, and frog. In these humorous tales, frog gets into all sorts of mischief.

> *The Silver Pony* by Lynd Ward is a long (83 pages) wordless picture book, appropriate for an older child, which tells the story of a lonely farm boy who takes imaginary trips all over the world on a winged horse.

Once a child can produce the oral language to accompany pictures, a basis has been established for understanding an author's printed language. The fact that print has meaning and corresponds closely to pictures, and tells a story just as oral language does, is important knowledge which successful readers possess.

Besides developing oral language, wordless picture books can be extremely useful for creating positive attitudes about books. For the child who is not reading or knows only a few words, these wordless texts can provide successful experiences with books. When reading pictures to tell the story, a child can say as much or as little as possible without a concern for correctly reading print. A child can successfully complete a picture reading task from which the possibility of failure with print has been removed. Good feelings about books, reading, and oneself can thus be created.

References

Abrahamson, R. F. "The Teaching of Composition Through Textless Books." Unpublished paper, University of Houston, 1977.

Alexander, Martha. *Out! Out! Out!* New York: Dial, 1968.

Anno, Mitsumasa. *Anno's Alphabet.* New York: Crowell, 1975.

Ardizzone, Edward. *The Wrong Side of the Bed.* Garden City: Doubleday, 1970.

Carle, Eric. *Do You Want to Be My Friend?* New York: Crowell, 1971.

D'Angelo, Karen. "Wordless Picture Books: Also for the Writer." *Language Arts,* 56, 7 (October 1979), 813–14, 835.

Degler, Lois S. "Putting Words into Wordless Books." *Reading Teacher,* 32, 4 (January 1979), 399–402.

Fuchs, Erich. *Journey to the Moon.* New York: Delacourt, 1969.

Goodall, John. *The Great Cat Chase.* New York: Harcourt, Brace, Jovanovich, 1968.

Hoban, Tana. *Big Ones, Little Ones.* New York: Greenwillow, 1976.

———. *Count and See.* New York: Macmillan, 1972.

Hogrogian, Nonny. *Apples.* New York: Macmillan, 1971.

Huck, C. S. *Children's Literature in the Elementary School.* New York: Holt, Rinehart & Winston, 1976.

Hutchins, Pat. *Changes, Changes.* New York: Collier, 1971.

Krahn, Fernando. *The Self-Made Snowman.* Philadelphia: Lippincott, 1974.

Larrick, Nancy. "Wordless Picture Books and the Teaching of Reading." *Reading Teacher,* 29, 8 (May 1976), 743–746.

Mari, Iela, and Mari, Enzo. *The Apple and the Moth.* New York: Pantheon, 1970.

———. *The Chicken and the Egg.* New York: Pantheon, 1969.

Mayer, Mercer. *Frog Goes to Dinner.* New York: Dial, 1974.

———. *Frog Where Are You?* New York: Dial, 1969.

Simmons, Ellie. *Family.* New York: McKay, 1970.

Spier, Peter. *Noah's Ark.* New York: Doubleday, 1977.

Sutherland, Z., and Arbuthnot, M. H. *Children and Books.* Glenview, Ill.: Scott, Foresman & Co., 1977.

Ueno, Noriko. *Elephant Buttons.* New York: Harper, 1973.

Ward, Lynd. *The Silver Pony.* Boston: Houghton Mifflin, 1973.

Attaining Sentence Verve with Sentence Extension

Flora Fennimore
Western Washington University

When the fourth graders came to me on that first September morning, they were all communicating verbally, meaning, of course, that they were talking and laughing and conveying their ideas with interest and enthusiasm. The challenge facing me was two-fold: teaching these students to transform the spoken message into a coherent written one, retaining and *increasing* its meaning and expressiveness; and achieving this goal, to some degree, with each student in a group with varied abilities (some normal learners, some intellectually impaired learners, and a few severely emotionally impaired learners).

One approach I used successfully was sentence extension. This tactic develops the student's ability to produce various kinds of words (action words, descriptive words, etc.) in response to sensory stimuli and in various syntactical arrangements (parts of the sentence, phrases, clauses, etc.). Sentence extension emphasizes the use of the parts of speech as well as the parts of a sentence.

Emphasizing the Parts of Speech

Practicing the Art Itself

Keeping in mind that I wanted to bring to the center of the classroom the daily experiences children have with words, feelings, and sentences, I introduced sentence extension on day one. My main objective was the idea of experiencing with the children various and, I hoped, more interesting ways to compose sentences while very indirectly teaching the parts of speech.

With the announcement "Let's work with some words now," I wrote the sentence "The boy ran" on the board. I then asked someone to read the sentence, making sure that I called the construction a sentence.

"In the sentence, 'The boy ran,' what words or nouns might we use in place of *boy*? Brainstorm."

50

Girl, child, person, children, and *grown up* were quickly supplied.

As the children furnished the responses shown in column three of Table 1, I copied them on the board.

"Good. You had no trouble thinking of plenty of nouns. Now, we have a 'pa' and an 'aunt' and an 'adult' and a 'monster' who 'ran.' This time, let's brainstorm for action words or verbs that we might use in place of *ran* so that we have these people doing actions other than running. For example, we might say 'The monster jumped.' "

"*Flew, rolled,* and *hopped,*" they responded.

And so the fourth graders supplied column 4 of Table 1. I wrote these words on the board in a column following the column of nouns to correspond with the usual order of the sentence parts in a sentence.

"Now we have a 'father' who 'galloped' or a 'grandfather' who 'scampered' " (pointing to the words in the various columns as I said them). "Let's see what we have when we brainstorm what kind of 'boy' or 'grandpa' or 'uncle' we are talking about. In other words, we want to think of describing words or adjectives, such as *large* to describe *boy.*"

Happy, sad, dumb, and the other colorfully descriptive words listed in column 2 of Table 1 emerged in the minute or two the children were allowed. Never were they given enough time in the production of any of the columns of responses to lose their enthusiasm. The words were listed in a column preceding the column of nouns to correspond with their proper sentence placement.

"Okay, now we have a 'dumb' 'baby' who 'galloped' or a 'grunty' 'monster' who 'fought' " (pointing to the words in the various columns). "Let's think how that 'grunty monster fought.' Did he fight *slowly* or *quickly* or *angrily?*"

"Pokey, slowly, and *like crazy,*" they replied.

Thus the adverbs in column 5, which were listed in a column following the verbs, were produced; and we were ready to consider the use of another adverbial modifier.

"Now we know that the 'grunty monster fought swiftly' " (pointing to the words in the various columns as I said them), "but we don't know how 'grunty' he was. Was he *very* grunty or was he *completely* grunty?"

After the children had produced a few adverbial modifiers designating the degree of gruntiness (column 1, Table 1), I quickly moved to a consideration of prepositional phrases.

"The 'very grunty monster fought swiftly' " (pointing to the words in the various columns). "Where did he 'fight swiftly?' Did he do it *under the barn* or *in the potato patch?*"

"Over the house! and *to China,*" they joined in.

Thus, the children created the prepositional phrases listed in column

Table 1

Children's Brainstorming for Sentence Extension

Sentence being extended: The boy ran.

1 →	2 →	3 ↗ ↘		4 →	5 →	6 →
very	happy	man	grandpa	flew	slowly	over a house
kind of	sad	men	grandma	rolled	fast	to China
mentally	dumb	pa	children	jumped	speedy	over the house
a little	nice	girl	grown up	walked	medium size	over his dog
	playful	child	monster	crawled	quickly	over the barn
	different	adult	cousin	skipped	very slowly	over the river
	weird	woman	granny	scampered	pokey	over the hose
	grumpy	aunt	old man	galloped	swiftly	over the fence
	retarded	baby	old lady	rode	like crazy	over a rock
	mad	uncle	ancestor	tore off		
	mean	niece	grandfather	slid		
	baby	person	mother	fought		
	grunty	father				
	stupid					

6. And again I recorded these responses on the board in the last column, to correspond with their usual placement in a sentence.

"Now let's see what our 'grunty monster' sentence sounds like with the explanation that he 'fought over the house.' 'The very grunty monster fought quickly over the house.' Now, who wants to try a sentence? Did you notice the small word or article, *the,* that I put at the beginning of the sentence? You may need to add an article to your sentence, too. What are the other two articles?"

After I had listed the articles in front of all the columns, Ian wanted to put a sentence together: "A kind of stupid old man slid pokey over a rock."

Giggles, waving hands, comprehending smiles, and eager looks emanated from the children; and Linda volunteered the second creation: "The weird girl galloped medium sized over the hose."

Following more chances to compose sentences using their conceived parts, the children proceeded with the assignment to write some sentences. Here is a sample of favorite sentences chosen by the students; all the children's writing included in this article is reproduced as they wrote it—that is, without corrections:

1. A little stiped man flew fast over a fence. Amy
2. Kind of happy old lady skipped very slowly over the rock. Tony
3. The play full granny jumped fast over the barn. Jerri
4. The very happy niece scampered quickly over the barn. Bill
5. The mentally retarded boy scampered very poky and triped over the hose. Sue
6. A mentally nice man walked swiftly over the dog. Lane
7. A little grumpy child scampered like crazy over a hole. Sharon
8. A little nice different child person crawled and scamperd like crazy very swiftly over the Barn. Alice
9. The very happy Old man and Old lady skipped fast over a hole. Tommy
10. The very grumpy man tore off like crazy over a rock. Bob

Several factors should be kept in mind about this first experience with sentence extension which occurred on the first day of school. One, sentence construction followed the developmental patterns of sentence sense learned by the children in language development. The topical questions for eliciting sentence parts were presented in the most logical and usual order in which a sentence is constructed, and the responses to those questions were listed on the board in the same sentence sequence. Sentence sense, thus, was attained by following the structure illustrated in Figure 1. And, because the responses were listed in the same order, sentence construction was attained by following the same structure—that given in the arrangement of sentence parts in Table 1.

Two, when I presented the topical questions to elicit parts of the sentence, I would often interchange the name of the desired part of speech for the description of that part of speech. For example, I would often request, "What words or nouns could we use in place of *boy*?" I practiced this habit not so much because I thought learning the parts of speech was necessary but because I thought learning them indirectly might be useful.

Three, as in brainstorming or any process of eliciting responses quickly, I terminated the children's production while the excitement was still high. If they could not produce with ease, as in the case of the responses in column 1 of Table 1, apparently they were not ready or responsive or alert.

Four, the words the children generated for sentence sources (Table 1) were reproduced and were filed in their binders for future use. They became descriptive dictionaries for the children when they needed words or when they needed word prompters.

Combining Sentence Extension with Creative Dramatics

For their second experience with sentence extension, the fourth graders assumed the role of the wind and, through a series of wind dramas, actually became the sentences they created.

"Today, we are going to be the wind. Stay in place and close your eyes if you want to. First, be any kind of wind, such as a breeze."

Responding by moving, hissing, and tearing, the children answered, after approximately 30 seconds of acting, that they were a "twister,"

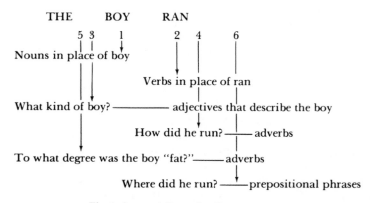

Fig. 1. Sentence Extension Structure

an "ice wind," or a "tornado" when I asked them what they were. These responses were listed on the board in a column as they gave them.

"This time let's all be the tornado that Joe was. Act as you think the tornado would act and then tell us the action you did. For example, you might be a tornado that 'thundered' or 'hissed' or 'jumped'." Again, after less than a minute of increasingly intense expression, I questioned how they acted. As you can see from the responses in Table 2, listed in a column to the right of the noun column, they were very active. They "knocked over trees," "lighteninged," and "broke up houses."

Table 2
Sentence Extension with the Wind

1. (adjectives)	2. (nouns)	3. (verbs)	4. (adverbs)	5. (prepositional phrases)
mad	twister	knocked over trees	interestingly	of the Empire State Building
slow	ice wind		stupidly	
fast	dust twister	turned over cars	strong	to the South
soft	storm		quickly	through water
quiet	sand storm	uprooted trees	slowly	to the East
sky	tornado	thundered	destructively	on the way to Kansas
strong		lighteninged	sparingly	
breezy		snowed	twisting	in Hawaii
tearing		rained	quickly	
frightening		hailed	furiously	
		picked up things		
		broke up houses		
		hurricaned		
		threw rocks		
		cleared land		
		tore tin		
		tore holes in the ground		

"As we become the tornado this time and 'thunder' or 'rain' or 'pick up things'" (pointing to their verbs on the board as I said them), "let's think how we would 'thunder' or 'pick up things.' Would you do it 'quickly' or 'dangerously'? Okay. Be the wind!"

For approximately a minute, they "hailed" and "cleared land" "interestingly" and "furiously" before they turned their attention to the kind of tornado they were as they were "hurricaning furiously." Their adverbial responses were recorded on the board as the third list follow-ing the verbs. In order to secure the adjectives to describe the kind of tornado each was, and the prepositional phrases to indicate where or for whom each was acting, I followed the same procedure as in the first sentence extension experience.

Having been intense, five-dimensional winds, the children settled down to the quiet aftermath of the storm to read and experiment in sentence form with the verbal descriptions that accompanied their actions. The almost mechanical production and transcription of words in the first experience (Table 1) was replaced on this day (Table 2) by human "tearing dust twister[s]" who "broke up houses furiously on the way to Kansas," by "breezy sand storm[s]" who "uprooted trees sparingly through water," and by "tearing ice wind[s]" who "tore holes in the ground interestingly in Hawaii." In this experience, emphasis was placed on the fact that the children's sentences were their talk written down; that the encouragement to alter, add, or combine words in sentences actually gave greater sentence sense or understanding; that assumption of a dramatic role in sentence construction resulted in greater dispersement of feelings; and that incorporation of sentence extension into drama actualizes the fact that writing is nothing but body talk that is transcribed from verbalizations (words) to writings (sentences).

Incorporating Sentence Extension into Prose Writing

Very little effort and time were expended in the classroom in developing sentence extension as a sterile entity, as occurred in the first experience. Incorporation of sentences is the essence, and incorporation in the chil-dren's prose writing is now our subject. To glean some, though sterile, comprehension of this operation, let us examine the lesson plan used with the pupils on their first day of prose writing (day two of the school year). The lesson combines sentence extension with prose writing:

1. "What are all the ways you can think of that you can travel from one place to another?" Possible responses to be recorded on board: *bike, car, plane, spaceship.*
2. Arbitrarily choose *spaceship.* "Let's take a spaceship and pre-tend it has landed in your back yard. What would you do if one landed in your yard?"
3. "If we were going to write about this spaceship landing in your back yard, what words would we use to describe the kind of spaceship that landed in your back yard?" Possible responses to

be recorded on the board: *scarey, big, bright orange, powerful, funny, gigantic.*

4. "Now, if you were to think of some action words that you might use in place of *landed,* what would you use?" Possible responses: *swooped, dived, jetted, darted, exploded.*
5. "Now, think of some words that tell how that 'gigantic' space-ship 'swooped'." Possible responses: *quickly, noisily, angrily.*
6. "The last words we want to think of are words that tell where the spaceship landed." Possible responses: *in the back yard, on the kitchen table, on your big toe, beside a bee.*
7. "Okay. Let's start a story together, of this spaceship landing in your back yard. How would you begin?" Record their story on the board.
8. Have them either finish this story or write a new one about a spaceship landing in their back yard. If they need words, they are to get them from me.

The goal was to motivate the children to express their thoughts in more colorful sentence composition. Question one elicited nouns or subjects of sentences or compositions. Personalization of the subject was achieved with question three, in which the children responded by describing with an adjective the specific spaceship that landed in each individual's back yard. Verbs or action words that might be more accurate or colorful for a *powerful* spaceship's landing were sought in question four. Prompter five requested words (adverbs) that described how that "gigantic" spaceship "swooped," and prompter six desired words (prepositional phrases) that told where the spaceship landed.

Variations of Sentence Extension

Building Sentences Individually

Sentence extension is not an isolated experience. Sentence sense is the sustenance of communication. From only a few years after birth, children are speaking and laughing and acting and singing and writing in sentences, whether they be one-worded or five-worded sentences. At some point, however, children need to take the time to name what they are doing so they can transfer the interestingly and colorfully spoken messages they have been communicating for years to the word of the page without losing their language's verve. This step is not an easy one. To assist in taking it, occasionally, very occasionally, I like to follow a sentence extension experience such as the one of the wind drama, with an assignment like the one shown in Table 3.

My directions for the assignment instructed the students, first, to write a simple sentence, such as "The cat ran." Then, the students were guided to think of words (nouns) to be inserted in the column numbered 1 that they might use in place of *cat,* of actions (verbs) the cat or any other noun they have listed might perform to be inserted in the column numbered 2, of words (adjectives) to describe the cat or any other nouns to be inserted in the column numbered 3, and so forth. The children clearly understood that no words in any column had to apply or be used in place of the words in the original sentence. After they had all the columns filled with approximately three to five words, they were to put the words together into sentences in any way they wanted to. I wish you could have the pleasure of examining the variety, quantity, and quality of the individual words and the sentences of each child. Instead, I have included a few examples of their sentences:

1. the pichblack Simesee cat slid veryfast over China
2. A paper white Simesee object slowly trotted over the hill.
3. The mediem black object walked noislessly toward the cave.
4. A regelar cream-color kitten trotted quietly up the walk.
5. a darck orenge cat jogged slowly over a mouse.
6. The gentle brown gerbil scampered quick on a cat.
7. A terribly Green squeaker jumped rapidly over the moon.
8. The very brown lame brain ran slowly off the earth.

Table 3

Sentence Extension Assignment

Sentence: The		cat		ran	.
		what you are talking about (noun)	action it did (verb)		
Words to describe how "black" the cat was (adverbs)	Words to describe the kind of cat it was (adjectives)	What we are talking about (noun)	Action words in place of *ran* (verbs)	Words that tell how the cat did his action (adverbs)	Words that tell where the cat did his action (prepositional phrase)
(5)	(3)	(1)	(2)	(4)	(6)

The fourth graders found an occasional assignment such as this one useful. In this frame of reference, they found little difficulty in learning new uses of parts of speech or of parts of a sentence, simply by enlarging on this basic sentence structure in any of the following ways: (1) by including additional word columns, such as a word (adverb) to describe how "pretty" or "tall" one was, (2) by combining two words in the subject or noun column to construct a sentence with a compound subject, (3) by combining two words in the verb column to construct a sentence with a compound verb or predicate, and (4) by combining two entire sentences with a coordinating conjunction to produce a compound sentence. Not all of these possibilities were discovered immediately; they were incorporated into sentence understanding as the year progressed.

Nonsensical Sentence Extension

"A few weeks ago you were the wind that erupted into a 'mad tornado' that 'lighteninged destructively to the South.' What element of nature do you want to be today?"

"Frost;" "the rain;" "fog;" "let's be what it's doing outside today—raining," they responded.

"Okay, the rain. First, act as you think the rain would. Drip or splash or beat. This time when you act as the rain, act out a nonsense action of the rain. For example, maybe the rain 'gafumped.' How would you act if you were rain 'gafumping'? Now, be the rain acting out the nonsense action you made up."

After a few minutes of flagellating rain spouts, I calmed the storm to discover that the children had been activated by such nonsensical verbs as *troomped, galooped,* and *blurbed.* From rains "blurbing" and "troomping" we proceeded to a discovery and dramatization of nonsensical words (adjectives) to describe the kind of rain we were, of nonsensical words (adverbs) to demonstrate to what degree we "galooped," and so forth. This experience is unlike the preceding sentence extension experiences only in its use of nonsense words: "The blangedly splorched rain brumlooped fittsodly over the blampf!"

Emphasizing the Parts of the Sentence

Emphasis on parts of the sentence rather than parts of speech can be attained simply by changing the schematic arrangement of prompters to the one shown in Figure 2.

In this experience, I usually commence by arbitrarily giving the children an enticing sentence and asking, in understandable terminology, what the complete subject and predicate are. Parceling of the complete subject and predicate is achieved by eliciting the simple subject and predicate and the corresponding modifiers. As this parceling is occurring, the children might be asked to think of other nouns that they might be talking about rather than *rains,* other verbs that might be used in place of *fall,* and so forth. Or, after the children have identified the parts of the sentence, they might divide into five groups and each group might brainstorm a different sentence part. Riotous sentences result when the children randomly contribute their sentence parts (Table 4). The mechanics of this sharing are usually achieved by having the children within the individual groups number off. Then, as I point to keep the action moving, number 1 in group 1 reads a noun; number 1 in group 2 adds a prepositional phrase; number 1 in group 3 adds a verb, and so forth. An infinity of sentences is created by each person adding a sentence part. "The rain in Spain" no longer "falls mainly on the plain," but "the sleezards at the recycling center tangerined weirdly within the feathers of a pillow."

A more sophisticated continuation or variation of the preceding experience would be one emphasizing the complete subject and predicate. For this endeavor, all the words brainstormed in the previous lesson (Table 4) would be reproduced on a mimeo. The children would be divided into two groups. The people in group 1 would be told they are assuming the role of the complete subject or the entire part of the

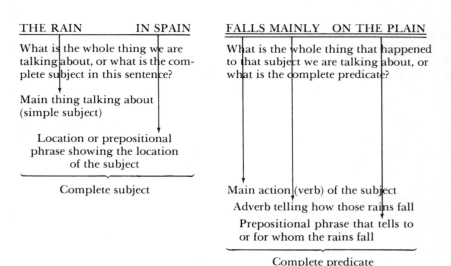

Figure 2. Sentence Extension Structure Emphasizing
the Parts of a Sentence

sentence telling what we are talking about, and group 2 would understand they are assuming the role of the complete predicate or the part of the sentence that gives the complete action of the subject. Person 1 from group 1 would supply any words from columns 1 and 2 (the complete

Table 4
The Rain in Spain Extended

The rain	in Spain	falls	mainly
gerbils	at a junction	collided	personally
sleezards	in the refriger-	addled	crazily
gumball	ator	aggravated	wildly
cookie dough	in the coffee tin	scrounged	weirdly
toe nail	on page three	limped	fantastically
caterpillars	by the slimy bog	languished	laughingly
diving board	near sewage	bomped	painlessly
slush	lagoon	galoomphed	tiredly
booze	at the recycling	tangerined	sensitively
mud	center	scooped	narrowly
	on a marsh-		
	mallow		
	on a stranger		
	in the phone		
	booth		

on the plain.	Some sentence combinations:
in peanut butter	1. The diving board in the phone booth collided laughingly within the feathers of a pillow.
in the aquarium	
around the wild things	
upon the edge of the pie crust	2. The cookie dough on page three scrounged sensitively around the wild things.
into the cookie dough	
in the sugar bowl	
inside a piece of chalk	3. The booze in the coffee tin bomped fantastically upon the edge of the pie crust.
within the feathers of a pillow	
beside the shoestring	
outside the blue hill	4. The slush at the recycling center limped weirdly in the sugar bowl.

Note: These responses are from children older than fourth grade. Occasionally, we became so absorbed in our process that we forgot to save the results for publication.

subject), and person 1 from group 2 would randomly supply any combination of words from columns 3, 4, and 5. Humorous and colorful sentences result from such a procedure, and the children have a greater understanding of sentence sense, particularly the elements of complete subject and predicate.

Potpourri

Experimentation with sentence sense begets sentence understanding. If you have as your objective and attitude the opening of the children as they are pursuing an understanding of sentence sense, then you will see growth. Suggestions for varied approaches for experiencing sentence extension are the following:

1. Rather than having the children number off by 5's or 6's for the parts of a sentence, have them choose the parts of the sentence they will be (a) by the name of the part of a sentence the child pulls out of a hat, or (b) by the color that characterizes the personality of the part of the sentence.

2. Have the sentence parts the children have composed put into six different boxes from which one child randomly will pull and read all his sentence parts or six different children will pull and read six parts.

3. Have the children in turn act out the sentences they compose. At first these can be planned sentences; later they can be the random variety suggested in number 2.

4. Put the sentence parts into boxes and have the children dramatize the results they draw.

5. Put the complete subjects of sentences the children have composed into one box and the complete predicates into another. Individual children in turn will draw out the two parts which they are to act out.

6. Number 5 can be varied by putting the six sentence parts into boxes and having the children dramatize the results they draw.

Summary

Sentence understanding is learned from infancy through use, not in isolation. In their talk and dramatic play, the fourth graders, in spite of their learning and emotional problems, used the various sentence parts. Sentence extension has been presented as a stimulus primarily in basic sentence structure, in an effort to (1) enliven and enhance the sentences the children speak with relative ease, (2) transcribe that talk into writing, and (3) create a repertoire of words they can call on. As children progress in sentence understanding, they can, as my fourth graders did, use this mechanical structure of sentence extension to learn more involved sentence structure (compound subjects, predicates, and sentences); sentence mechanics (punctuation and capitalization); and composition (monologue, dialogue, exposition, and drama).

Special Needs That Don't "Squeak": Freeing Students from the Bonds of Reticence

Don Rubin
The University of Georgia

Each and every student has special needs. We know that, and we do our best to meet them within practical constraints. But some students are so challenged by educational environments that properly serving them requires major revision in classroom management. Sometimes we have difficulty diagnosing the exact nature of these students' needs. But if a sixth-grade student isn't reading a word, if a first-grader is violently abusive, if a teenager consistently nods out in class, we at least perceive that a problem exists. "The squeaky wheel gets oiled," a colleague recently reminded me.

Sitting in our classes is a group of students who have a disability, and because they do not "squeak," it is easy to ignore their special needs. That they do not call attention to themselves is part and parcel of their problem. That years of experience have reinforced their disability makes it especially difficult to reach these individuals. That they will perform beneath their potential and suffer personal discomfort so long as this disability persists makes it imperative that we do reach them. If we attune ourselves to this condition as a handicap, we will easily recognize who these students are. They are the quiet ones, the reticent ones.

Does reticence truly qualify as a "special need"? Students may remain quiet in a classroom for a variety of reasons. Some may be chronically unprepared, and smart enough not to flaunt the matter. But the person who is disposed to avoid interpersonal interaction in general is in serious trouble. Evidence suggests that such students do not do as well in school as they ought (reticence is not related to ability), that they will be perceived as unattractive individuals by their peers, that this trait will affect their life-style and mating choice, and that it will ultimately affect their careers—because of their own selection of low-profile, low-prestige positions and also because of employers' negative assessments.

Reticence is an umbrella term that covers a range of speech avoidance syndromes. What is common among reticent individuals is fear or discomfort in communicating in many situations, and not just in those situations which perhaps rightly inspire anxiety. (Stage fright is a normal response to public speaking, not a symptom of reticence.) Reticence is a learned trait, acquired by some youngsters who are sensitive to being punished for speaking up, rewarded for being "nice and quiet." It is an all too common disability. In a class of thirty you can expect to find six students who experience dysfunctional levels of communication apprehension. Two resources which pertain to reticence deserve careful reading by educators: *Quiet Children and the Classroom Teacher* by James McCroskey (ERIC Clearinghouse on Reading and Communication Skills, 1977; available from NCTE or the Speech Communication Association) and *Shyness and Reticence in Students* by Paul Friedman (National Education Association, 1980).

The following activity is a form of systematic desensitization, moving from low to high threat communication situations. It can be used—and used repeatedly—at all grade levels. The primary objectives of this exercise are to give students a history of success in communicating before others and to promote a classroom atmosphere in which talk is valued. I have found that it is most effective when the teacher takes the first risk and sets an attainable model by fully participating.

Students are given a homework assignment that asks them to think of a personal anecdote, a brief narrative, which they can share with the class. I sometimes give as an example the story of a nonstop cross-country drive I took in college. With only limited time available for the trip, my friends and I subsisted for 2,000 miles on candy bars and cokes. We arrived before dawn at our destination in Seattle, craving anything approaching real food. The craving was especially accentuated because our host was famed as a magnificent cook. While I spread sleeping bags in the living room, I heard loud crunching issuing from the still dark kitchen. David called out, "These are the best chocolate chip cookies I've ever tasted." I eagerly joined in and concurred with the view. It wasn't until we awoke in midafternoon that we learned there had been no cookies on the counter, only a bowl of dog food.

Students pair off and tell their stories to their partners. Then the partners join a small group of two other pairs, and all members again tell their stories. Often partners will prompt and encourage each other. Finally, the class forms a semicircle with two chairs placed at the focal point. (Or, in the upper grades, this may be taken as an opportunity for a stand-up speech.) Each set of partners takes its place as story tellers. After each story the class applauds, spontaneously one hopes.

This simple procedure has several advantages. Having partners go before the class together gives the story teller support and decreases that feeling of being the sole center of attention. By the time students are ready to tell the story for the third time, they are no longer worrying about what they are going to say. Also, they have the opportunity to engage in a kind of revision process. Typically, students will shift into slightly more formal registers by choosing more descriptive language and enunciating more clearly as they move into larger groups. One point of discussion afterwards can focus on how the students spoke differently in the three situations. The other major point, of course, focuses on how they felt differently. In addition, the exercise is a good opportunity to discuss what makes some stories especially interesting. The discussion may evince the following criteria: (1) a good story creates a setting, (2) it goes someplace, has a climax, or makes a point, and (3) it includes detail and elaboration. (Digressions are acceptable in this genre.) A final advantage of this activity is that telling and listening to these personal anecdotes is pleasurable.

And that is the way talk ought to be, for all.

Classmates Together, Generations Apart

Peter M. Schiff
Northern Kentucky University

It was not many years ago that my high school seniors were all seventeen or eighteen years old when school started each September. My college freshmen were eighteen or nineteen. Now, students seeking adult learning center high school equivalency diplomas or beginning community college and four-year university degree programs are not necessarily teenagers. They may be Vietnam era veterans returning to school in their late twenties, women seeking to reenter the job market in their thirties and forties, or all sorts of people in their fifties, sixties, and beyond who desire the formal education they did not obtain earlier in life.

In return for the English portion of this schooling, our "new," older students offer us experience-shaped insights into language usage, fictional characters' behavior, and untapped sources of composition topics. For the English teacher, however, fostering such classroom contributions poses challenges.

Many students who have been out of school for a number of years are frightened of participating in discussions. They may worry about "wrong" answers jeopardizing "last chances" for academic success. Or, they may dread being called "out-of-date," "just like my parents," or even "hypocritical" by their younger classmates.

It is the instructor's responsibility to draw older pupils into the mainstream of class discussion and to raise all students' awareness of the communication-inhibiting biases they may bring to dealings with classmates of different generations. Used very early in the term, the following five-activity language arts lesson can promote frequent, sensitive classroom communication.

Activity #1 (Viewing). The instructor shows the class a film, poster, or photograph whose content might stereotypically be expected to stir controversy along generational lines. Examples of such stimuli include: *Claude*, a short animated film that depicts a young child's harassment by (and revenge upon) his nagging parents; a poster calling for raising the legal drinking age to twenty-one or lowering it to eighteen; photographs of screaming teenagers at a rock concert, businesspeople in three-piece or tailored tweed suits, and patients in nursing homes. After viewing the film, poster, or photograph, students jot down reactions to the visual stimuli.

Activity #2 (Speaking/Listening). Students take a few minutes to reflect upon their jottings. Then they tell the class their reactions to what they have seen. These reactions usually take the form of opinions for or against the perceived message of the visual stimulus. Before offering a reaction, a student must restate the previous pupil's statement to that pupil's satisfaction. This technique, an adaptation of one used by psychologist Carl Rogers (1961, pp. 329–337), provides training in the oft-forgotten skill of listening. Aural practice also alerts students to the teacher's concern for classroom communication based upon the actual statements of classmates.

Activity #3 (Writing). In two writing sessions of five minutes each, pupils are asked to write down (1) what they expected to hear from the classmate who spoke just before they did (the first speaker reacts to the last), and (2) what they actually heard. When younger and older students write about each other, results of writing sessions #1 and #2 may be (1) identical, as in one older student's fulfilled expectation that an eighteen-year-old classmate would vehemently oppose raising the drinking-age, (2) totally opposite, as in a younger pupil's surprise at finding an older classmate supportive of encouraging rock concerts in a local arena, or (3) partly similar, partly different, as in both younger and older students' ambivalent feelings about nursing home confinement and care.

Activity #4 (Reading). Students receive fifteen minutes for sharing their writing from Activity #3 with classmates. Reading is silent, with students getting to see as many writings as possible in the alloted time.

Activity #5 (Synthesizing). Students receive index cards on which they write a series of statements reacting to the viewing, speaking/listening, writing, and reading activities. Helpful ways to begin such statements are suggested by Simon, et al. (1972, pp. 163–165). These include, "I learned that . . .," "I realized that I . . .," "I relearned that I . . .," "I noticed that I . . .," "I discovered that I . . .," "I was surprised that I . . .," "I was pleased that I . . .," and "I was displeased that I . . . ."

Pupils who have engaged in this language arts lesson have made the following statements:

"I learned that teenagers can be concerned about older people."

"I learned that people under thirty often prejudge those over thirty."

"I discovered that I enjoyed listening to what some of these young people had to say."

"I was displeased that students my children's age wanted to treat me like an unsympathetic parent."

"I noticed that no one made fun of me or put me down when I expressed my opinion." (an older student)

Shared with the class at large, these and similar reactions have helped set a tone that encourages thoughtful, willing response from both traditionally aged and older students. The realizations expressed in the "I learned . . ." statements also nurtured self- and inter-generational understanding leading to (1) insightful discussion of short stories involving conflict (e.g., John Updike's "The Lucid Eye in Silver Town," dealing with father-son relationships; Sarah Orne Jewett's "The Courting of Sister Wisby," treating differences between two generations of women), (2) intriguing compositions in which students wrote about current issues from the points of view of their past, present, and future selves, and (3) provocative argument over points of language usage (e.g., current slang vs. past slang; the disappearance of "whom" as the objective case of the relative pronoun).

One particularly appealing feature of this lesson is that it does not formally ask older pupils to respond to younger, or vice versa. Rather, students communicate with students. The "I learned . . ." statements listed above were only a few of many such reactions, most of which had nothing to do with older and younger students' perceptions of one another. That the students whose statements are cited reached their conclusions by themselves indicates that the five-part language arts lesson aided a delicate, seemingly contradictory process. On the one hand, the lesson mainstreamed nontraditional pupils into the give and take of classroom discussion. On the other, it highlighted those students' values as individual, rather than as stereotypical of older generations.

References

Rogers, Carl R. *On Becoming a Person.* Boston: Houghton Mifflin Co., 1961.

Simon, Sidney B., Howe, Leland W., and Kirschenbaum, Howard. *Values Clarification: A Handbook of Practical Strategies for Teachers and Students.* New York: Hart Publishing Co., 1972.

3 Minority Students and Non-Native Speakers

Teaching Gay Students

Louie Crew
University of Wisconsin, Stevens Point

Gay students are ubiquitous, yet no attention has been given to their special needs or to the skills required of those who would teach them. As a gay person, I have a special interest in redressing this widespread professional neglect. I believe that gay students should be taught the way other students should be taught. That is, unless the teacher is some kind of sadist, one teaches students to survive and to thrive as who they are, not as who they are not, and to thrive in this culture rather than in some other. It follows that to be minimally competent to teach gay students, one must know the gay experience in the adult world.

I am not suggesting that we should all go study gay bars or gay churches or the like, although such visitations could be extremely instructive for sensitive observers. Certainly books are a very limited substitute for studying foreign experience, particularly taboo experience, because the taboos that affect the experience typically affect the presentations of that experience in books, on television, and in the movies. Gay writers are regularly rewarded either for masking their experience as nongay or for telling it as gay but in terms that reassure nongays in their condemnation of the gay experience. The media distort typically by ignoring gay experience altogether, as do most teachers, talking always as if everyone shared the nongay orientation. Notions to the contrary notwithstanding, gays are not like nongay readers, at least not in several important respects, many of which are not specifically genital. Any teaching that denies or ignores our differences fails by that ignorance to educate us, to lead us out into a full awareness of our own potentials for thriving as we are in this world.

Instead of urging teachers to come into the gay world, I am urging acknowledgment of the gay experience in the world we share and asking that these gay dimensions be treated seriously, lovingly. Much that we already teach offers opportunities for such acknowledgment. For example, in teaching *The Scarlet Letter*, no one has failed to discuss in detail the taboo of heterosexual adultery at the heart of the book. Certainly anyone sensitive to the gay experience of taboo recognizes some strong parallels in the health and guiltlessness that declosseted and vulnerable Hester experiences, in contrast to the psychic destruction and sense of sin that closeted Arthur experiences, both in response to the same erotic act. Already some gays have turned their scarlet Q's from "Queer" into "Queen" as an ameliorative linguistic thrust; and any sensitive lexicographer, of whom there seem to be precious few, must now record that in the experience of increasing numbers of us, "gay" no longer means "dissolute," "giddy," or any of the other negative associations of the word we have selected as our name for ourselves.

Yet how many teachers will admit gay insight openly into classroom discussions of such books as *The Scarlet Letter,* much less allow gay students the prerogative of using their own language? How many teachers create a climate of academic inquiry where one would even want to share insight? When was the last time one heard "Eureka!" in the academy? I have the feeling that libraries would fall tumbling down if anyone were to make an audibly joyful discovery in them anymore.

The kinds of gay discovery I am discussing will not mean the bringing of greater looseness into academic discussions. I am not urging (even if maybe I should) that teachers use any more explicit detail than they already employ for heterosexual reality. I do not normally take it that a nongay has performed a sex act in class when citing his or her role as mother or father. When I refer to my lover or spouse of the same sex, I am making a standard reference with no specifically genital or political detail. If one sees genitals or hears politics, those are not my problems. I simply cannot take responsibility for having named unspeakable orgies that go on in nongay heads. My lover and I and all of our gay colleagues and students are going to need to be especially strong to survive such distortions.

No one should pity gay students or go especially easy on them. In loving ways strong teachers, nongay and gay alike, should seize the already heightened sensitivity of most gay students and show them creative, non-neurotic ways to channel talents and energies, while at the same time joining the battle against the ignorance that makes gays, especially younger gays, such ready prey to nongay predators. I would hope that nongay adults would soon grow to realize that gays often experience the greatest persecution at home by insensitive parents or by parents who have wrongly indicted themselves for having "caused" such anomalies.

Lacking "gay family," gay students often need the structures of educational institutions more than anyone else. Very much needed are ways in which young gays can meet other gays, particularly gay professionals and other adults who demonstrate what otherwise they have never been allowed to see: that gay people can and do thrive, even in the open and even facing some rather incredible forms of persecution. I would hope too that teachers would be more in touch with gay history and gay literature and able to talk more comfortably about them in all standard courses, where they really belong if those courses are to be complete and honest.

The most meaningful letter of the scores that I have received about the special issue of *College English* on "The Homosexual Imagination" (November 1974), which I coedited with Rictor Norton, was from the mother of a gay teenager, thanking us for giving her more ammunition to help her help her son in his battle for survival. Would that all gay youngsters were so fortunate as to have such understanding and support!

Recently a very troubled gay first-year student sat next to me and whispered: "Girl, let me tell you what awful happened to me last week."

"Sure, dear," I comforted.

"I was on the line for a fraternity and missed one meeting. When I came the next day they said, 'We had to work; don't you think you should have to work too?' 'Sure,' I said; 'you ran a mile; I'll even run two miles.' 'No,' they said; 'you're going to perform fellatio on all 13 of us.'"

"You didn't let them get away with it!" I interrupted.

"But they wouldn't let me in their fraternity!" he moaned.

"But they weren't going to let you in the fraternity anyway, don't you see. And that's not a fraternity worth being in. They don't know the meaning of the word," I said.

"Oh, they would have let me in if I had done so," he replied, "only they would have had something on me and would have used me more. It's just not a sissy's world; now I am in nobody's group."

No amount of protest to remove that fraternity from our college—a protest that this student does not want, as it would make him even more vulnerable—will remove this brilliant young man's problem. His parents refuse to see that he's gay and he knows that they are horrified that he even *might* be. Many gay students perceive him to be weaker than they can risk in an associate. His college, his church, and his town provide only the most sordid conditions in which he can meet others who share his biological urges and where he can try to build complete, as opposed to merely biological, relationships. Efforts even to get a room for a group of gay students to use in meeting to discuss such problems have been thwarted with great shows of administrative power at the College and at a nearby church, which offers its facilities to most other secular groups requesting the use of them.

Clearly this young man needs to learn that there are persons, gay persons, who can reciprocate his affection in full relationships, and he deserves the same institutional supports provided for nongays passing through the crucial period of growing up and learning to reach out to others. Some require dances. Some use church occasions, or picnics, or hayrides. Some require marriage counseling (or in gay terms, lover counseling). Surely all are well served by a fair and complete range of presentation of their experience in literature, the movies, and on television. When was the time that we have seen something so innocuous in the media as a goodbye kiss by a same-sex couple when one of them is leaving for work? Believe me, such small moments of affection and support happen all the time in our world; and no one needs to be shielded from this kind of reality.

Equally disturbing, if not more so, are the perverted notions of human relations held by the 13 self-styled nongays who brutalized the young man on this occasion. I am wondering what sort of sharing they would be able to bring even to a heterosexual relationship. I suspect that they are beyond redemption. Perhaps the one positive result of this experience for the gay student, and it was slim pickings indeed, was that he could sit down with a gay professor whom he respected, who had known some of the same rejection, and say, "Hey, girl . . ." and spill out his heart. Clearly he is going to need more internal strength and support to compensate for the lack of structure elsewhere if he is to thrive as who he is. I would like to think that all gays are stronger than all nongays precisely because we face more rigorous challenges that require independence. But I fear that more are crushed than are proved strong by the harsh realities gays face in their persecution by nongays.

I hope that most people now know that many gay colleagues have faced just such severe intimidation and have later become, in diverse ways, strong, mature, and productive adults. If one does not know such gays in one's midst, it is only because that midst has not been made a safe place in which gays can share the fact of these victories. If most people now know that the gay community is far more diverse than most stereotypes admit, nevertheless every time I write or speak I have in my audience some for whom the occasion is their first experience knowingly confronting a gay person or a gay point of view. I tremble lest anyone assume that I could or would want to represent all gay people or all of gay experience. We gay people reflect this fear of someone else's speaking for us more strongly than do nongays: "Lord, I hope people won't think he's describing me! Why I would never allow another gay male to call me 'Girl' . . ." thinks the closeted gay male chairperson reading this article right now. And of course I am not.

In the past gays have learned to survive mainly by pretense and by subterfuge, at a sacrifice much too grave and unjust, not only to ourselves but to our families and the culture we might more richly have served. Today we ask to be allowed, even taught, to thrive as the large and important minority that we are. The biggest problems that we gays face are the fears nongay people have of us. The fact that as a colleague I can say this to nongays gives me hope that at last we may begin mutually to discover solutions.

Journal Writing for Non-Native Speakers of English

Leslie Tsimbos
Delta College, University Center, Michigan

One of the monumental tasks of the teacher of English to non-native speakers is bridging the gap between the students' thought processes, which occur in the native language, and the development of fluency in English. While this linguistic mental adjustment on the part of the learners is a gradual one, asking ESL students (speakers of English as a second language) to keep a journal in English is one effective means of hastening the attainment of communicative competence, and often includes other benefits as well.

It is important to stress to the students that this journal is first and foremost their own personal record, and no one except the teacher will read it unless they themselves wish to share it with others. I encourage the students to record in their journal notebooks their thoughts, feelings, questions, joys, disappointments, etc., as opposed to a mere catalogue of day-by-day events. In time, many learners come to regard the journal as a confidant to which they can express opinions they might never feel free to verbalize in English.

Next, in introducing the journal assignment, a target number of words should be set as a daily writing goal. Teen-aged or adult, high beginner/low intermediate ESL students can produce 50 words a day in their journals without any great difficulty; high intermediate/advanced students can write around 100 words a day as a reasonable assignment. It should be pointed out that this quantity of writing is an approximation, and that on some days the students may have lots to say and so write 150 or 200 words easily, while on other days even 40 words may be hard to find. Certainly the teacher is not going to count every word in each journal entry, but it is important to require an "average" number of words as the daily goal.

Perhaps most important of all is the teacher's stipulation that the students' journal writings be done without concern for correctness in spelling, grammar, punctuation, and the like. The students should be encouraged to write rapidly and freely, trying as best they can to communicate ideas and feelings in English without worrying about how "correct" the writing is or how many mistakes the teacher will find.

In the beginning, the teacher should check the journals frequently to ensure that the students write every day, on any topic they choose to explore. Once the journal is well established as a daily assignment it can be turned in for evaluation less frequently (every two weeks, perhaps). In checking the journal, the teacher should read each entry and try to write a short, appropriate response to what the student has written. Expressions of sympathy for disappointments, explanations to questions, requests for more information, congratulations for happy occasions, etc., should be written by the teacher directly on the journal pages, in reaction to what the student has said there.

The journal becomes, then, a form of private correspondence between student and teacher in which an invaluable rapport between the two can be quickly established. The only correction which the teacher should make in the journal is to supply occasional English vocabulary or idioms to better express the student's meaning in a given context, and even these should be done as little as possible. The aim of the journal is to encourage the learners to communicate in English in a sympathetic, supportive, and nonjudgmental environment, not to reinforce the fear that English is impossible to learn—a fear which is often substantiated by writing assignments handed back, covered with red pencil marks.

The main advantage of the ESL journal, I have found, is that it encourages "real" communication in English between the student and the teacher. Classroom drills and exercises, while necessary, are artificial language situations usually carried out in a demand/response context. In the journal, the students have the freedom to choose topics which have the most interest or relevance for them, without great regard for level of difficulty since correctness of expression is not a criterion for grading the journal assignments. By giving permission to make mistakes, the journal helps develop freedom of expression and the courage to take risks in communicating in English—both essential if the students are ever to move beyond "workbook" language and become comfortably proficient in English.

Another advantage of the journal is the insight it affords the teacher in regard to the students' personal lives. For learners from cultures in which a teacher is regarded as a highly respected (and thus unapproachable) authority figure, the journal acts as an intermediary means of expressing personal feelings which might be impossible in a face-to-face confrontation, no matter how open and accessible the teacher may try to be. Through the journal I have often gained valuable information about my students' families, home life, past difficulties, and current problems, which has helped me to view my students more realistically and more sympathetically. A word of caution should be given, however, about accepting everything in the journal at face value. Some students enjoy using the journal for flights of fancy or to imagine tragic or dramatic situations in which they are the victim/hero/heroine. Certainly this is permissible and even desirable under the scope of the assignment, but the teacher should take care not to jump to conclusions about the students solely on the basis of their journal writings.

Additionally, I believe the journal provides ESL students with a means to develop some kind of conceptual framework in which to fit their experiences in their new and sometimes incomprehensible environment. The fact that the students know that their journals will be thoughtfully read and commented on encourages attempts to write clearly. At the same time, the journal provides a needed outlet for expression of the frustrations and triumphs of adjusting to life in an alien culture. At the end of a semester, can students doubt their progress in ESL when they can look back on five or ten thousand words they have managed to write in their journals—especially since their teacher has responded in turn to the ideas and emotions they have expressed? In effect, the writing journal is proof to both student and teacher that meaningful communication in English is not an intangible future goal, but rather an accomplished fact.

Finally, for students of ESL trying desperately to keep up with a class of American students, the journal is one way to build confidence in their ability to succeed by providing a quantitative instead of qualitative basis for grading. Surely a teacher whose ESL students faithfully fulfill the journal assignment can feel justified in rewarding their dedication and perseverance with an A for effort, even when the same students perform inadequately when competing with their American classmates in other assignments.

The old adage that "Nothing succeeds like success" is certainly as true when applied to ESL students as to businesspeople. I have ample evidence from my own experience to support my belief that the journal is an excellent means of convincing students of their own ability to succeed as learners of English as a second language, and, eventually, to attain full communicative competence in English.

Comprehension and the Limited English Speaker

Nancy J. House
Billings Elementary School, Missouri

Many children who originally speak a language other than English have little initial trouble in learning to read in their second language. It is only as these children reach third or fourth grade that they begin to have difficulty. They can still decode the words, but no longer have complete understanding of the meaning being conveyed. The vocabulary and informational and conceptual loads carried by the printed page have become too complex for them. In social studies, science, and health, limited English speakers decode words, sentences, paragraphs, and whole pages with little comprehension.

Classroom teachers working with these children in the early grades sometimes unwittingly add to the problem by emphasizing and re-emphasizing the decoding skills while expecting comprehension to occur naturally. One reason for this is that their evaluation as teachers by both parents and principals is often based on the ability of children to pick up a book and orally reproduce the sounds symbolized on the written page. Another reason for stressing decoding is that it is relatively easy to teach. There are countless books outlining the necessary skills, and the sequence and techniques to follow in presenting them.

The same cannot be said for comprehension skills, perhaps because reading comprehension is not a separate entity. Connor (1978) has found a positive correlation between the listening and reading skills of learners who speak English as a second language (ESL). For once a child has learned to decode words, much of reading comprehension is based on an understanding of oral language, but this is a more nebulous area in which to work. Skills such as listing supporting detail, making inferences, or analyzing and synthesizing information are not all that easy to teach, while developing vocabulary could be an endless task. Still, the difficulty of working in the area of comprehension is equaled only by the importance of doing so. This article discusses techniques for developing comprehension in ESL children (who are invariably, at one time or another, limited English speakers).

Lexical Access

It almost goes without saying that lexical access, or vocabulary development, is the base upon which all comprehension is built. Few children lack basic experiences even if they are vicarious ones obtained from watching television. What they do lack are labels on these experiences and links between them. In kindergarten and first grade, teachers may encourage the development of these labels through the use of pictures to spark class discussions and help the children to develop their *hearing* vocabulary.

Books have long been one of the best mediums for the extension of lexical access. Researchers such as Greenlaw, Seaton, and Fisher (1977), Chomsky (1972), and Cohen (1968) report that literature has an effect on vocabulary growth and reading achievement. For the ESL child who has not yet mastered the decoding skills, or has mastered them but does not care to read voluntarily, the teacher has a powerful tool in the traditional "story time." That fifteen minutes or so after recess, when the teacher reads to the class, can be used to reap benefits in extended vocabulary development. The books read, however, should be works of children's literature that use language in a sophisticated manner such as Caldecott and Newbery award winners, and the like. A story time with the purpose of developing vocabulary is appropriate throughout the elementary grades. In addition, after a book has been read, the teacher can set it out where those who are able to do so may read it for themselves.

Children more rapidly associate words with people than with things. They also learn new vocabulary in short, meaningful experiences which makes the dramatization of word meanings an effective technique. Plays and reader's theater allow children to simultaneously practice decoding skills and develop vocabulary. Instead of spending large amounts of time having children memorize the lines to a play, have them act out the play with the script in their hands. This means children could do several plays in the time it usually takes to prepare just one. It means they will have been exposed to that much more use of language. (Of course, with reader's theater the children automatically read from a script.) The teacher can enhance the children's assimilation of new vocabulary by asking questions related to both the actors and the audience's understanding of each production.

In the primary grades, the traditional "sharing" or "show and tell" time can be used to extend and develop vocabulary. It is the teacher who must foster this by asking appropriate questions and drawing out definitions and explanations. When vocabulary is introduced in reference to the ideas children express, the vocabulary is personalized and thus more meaningful.

Many times teachers shy away from precise or exotic words because "The children won't understand what I am saying." Actually, it makes good sense for teachers to frequently talk "above" the children and then provide, or elicit from the class, a definition or understanding of what has been said.

Brief, noneducational comments made to individual ESL children will also extend their vocabularies if the teacher remembers to use appropriate language. When little Maria or Juan hears, "I like your *plaid* coat," a new word is added to the child's repertoire.

The least effective way to develop vocabulary, even with those older ESL children who speak and read English fairly well, is to send them to the dictionary. Adults use a dictionary only as a last resort when they cannot get the meaning of a word from the context in which it is used or by asking a friend for a definition. Why then should teachers expect children to be eager to learn vocabulary in such a manner? Also, dictionaries lack immediate application and do not provide an opportunity to use words in speech.

Syntax

Besides lexical access or vocabulary development, ESL children need an understanding of English syntax or how words are strung together to provide meaning. As any classroom teacher will attest, these children spend a lot of time talking. But careful listening to their conversations indicates they often speak to each other in their native language. Also, when they do converse in English they frequently speak in short phrases, use improper verb tenses, or at best, use very brief and simple sentences. Teachers do not help matters by accepting answers to questions, or comments on activities, that are poorly phrased. It takes extra class time, but children benefit from having to speak in complete sentences when saying something before, or to, the teacher or the rest of the class.

Prepositions. ESL children are often confused as to the meanings conveyed by prepositions. The sentence, "The spider ran _____ the box," can be used to illustrate almost any preposition except *of* (*under, over, on, behind,* etc.). To graphically clarify the various meanings of the sentence, a box and a rubber spider from the toy store may be positioned as the changing prepositions dictate. Imagine the laughter as a child demonstrates, "The spider ran *with* the box," or "The spider ran *after* the box." To allow each child in the class to become totally involved, the teacher could pass out dittoed papers with a box drawn on them or give the children actual small boxes. The students could then manipulate spiders, which they have previously sketched on paper and cut out, *above, below,* or *across* the box as indicated by the prepositions. For variety, it could be stated, "The child ran _____ the table," which would allow individual children to act out the changing sentence.

Adjectives. To develop the uses and meanings of adjectives, the teacher can put "The _____ boy is very _____," on the board and ask for words to place in the blanks. To vary things, the subject may be altered such as, "The _____ dragon is very _____." For more elaborate practice, try "The _____, _____ dragon is very _____ and _____." Of course, the various sentences that are made should always be read aloud. When children are comfortable using interesting and exciting adjectives in speech, such words begin to appear in their independent writing—for speech comes first, and children can only write what they can say.

Sequence. The sequence in which events occur can confuse ESL children. *When* something happens is often signified by a single word or phrase which these children may overlook. The teacher can write sentences such as the following on strips of paper, and place the strips in a pocket chart:

> While eating the princess, the dragon became ill.
> After climbing the ladder, the fireman rescued the dog.
> Before singing a song, the performer tuned his guitar.
> During the movie, Sue fell asleep.

Next to each sentence, individual children place cards which read "same time" or "different time" depending on when the two activities in a sentence happen. For those sentences in which the two activities occurred at different times, the children label (with the numbers 1 and 2) each activity, designating which one occurred first and which one second. Thus, they become aware of key words (*while, after, before,* and *during*) in the sample sentences.

When this activity has been mastered, the teacher may give the children cards or dittoed papers on which a series of directions has been written. The children read the directions, and then one child acts them out while the other children in the group or class watch to see if the proper sequence is used. Two examples, one simple and one more complex, of such directions are:

1. Before shaking your friend's hand, stand up.
2. While sitting down, touch your head. Then stand up and turn around. After this, sit down again. Finally, smile at the teacher.

Another activity to bring to the attention of children the sequence in which things happen is for the teacher to write a short story with individual sentences on separate pieces of heavy paper. Each child, or group of children, has a story which must be put together in the proper order. The sentences may be numbered on the back so children can check themselves as to whether they achieve the correct order. However, the first time a child or group puts a story together, the arrangement of the sentences which is decided upon should then be evaluated with the teacher and the class as a whole. If the sequence is incorrect, there should be discussion about why it is incorrect. A sample of the kind of story which may be used is as follows:

1. Mother has had a busy day.
2. Before she ironed, she had to wash the clothes.
3. Then she went to the store for groceries.
4. She was back when John came home from school, and took him to the doctor for a checkup.
5. Now she is making dinner.

To make the stories more attractive, the teacher can cut out interesting magazine pictures and mount them on heavy paper. Then stories written about these pictures may be assembled next to them.

Punctuation and Reading with "Expression." ESL children need to become aware that punctuation in writing, and the tone of voice and pauses in oral speech, carry meaning. Two sentences may be put together for children to punctuate, such as:

Sue will drive the car in the house Tom is napping

Where the periods are placed is vitally important to the meaning of these sentences:

Sue will drive the car in the house. Tom is napping.
Sue will drive the car. In the house Tom is napping.

The next step is for a reader to group the words in these sentences in a way that conveys meaning. The words must be orally grouped into meaningful phrases and read with what used to be called "expression." The two sentences above could be grouped as follows:

Sue will drive the car./ In the house/Tom is napping./

The teacher can provide totally unpunctuated paragraphs which are within the decoding ability of ESL children. Each child should silently read the paragraph and decide where the punctuation and/or phrasing belongs. After marking it in, the children can take turns reading their paragraphs to the group, which listens critically to see if the reader is accurately conveying the meaning by voice. Different meanings conveyed by different phrasing or emphasis may be compared and contrasted.

For instance, the following sentence changes its meaning depending upon which word is emphasized:

> *I* never mentioned I ate your chocolate cookie.
> I *never* mentioned I ate your chocolate cookie.
> I never *mentioned* I ate your chocolate cookie.
> I never mentioned *I* ate your chocolate cookie.
> I never mentioned I *ate* your chocolate cookie.
> I never mentioned I ate *your* chocolate cookie.
> I never mentioned I ate your *chocolate* cookie.
> I never mentioned I ate your chocolate *cookie.*

A discussion of sentences such as this will help children to learn how to "read between the lines," to analyze and evaluate meanings.

Main Idea and Supporting Detail. To enable even young ESL children to understand the difference between a main idea and supporting detail, the teacher could ask, "What is the most important thing to you right now?" If a child answers, for instance, "recess," the teacher asks the class to give several reasons why recess is important to them. These reasons are listed on the board such as:

> *Recess*
> On a basketball team
> Like to play with my friends
> Get to use the restroom
> Get exercise

Then the teacher can ask, "What else is important to you right now?" If a child answers, "my birthday," the class may offer a number of reasons why birthdays are important:

> *Birthdays*
> Get presents
> Have a party
> Am a year older

Then the teacher can say, "Let's label 'recess' and 'birthdays' *I* and *II*, and let's call the reasons under them *A, B,* and *C,* like this:"

I. Recess
   A. On a basketball team
   B. Like to play with my friends
   C. Get to use the restroom
   D. Get exercise
II. Birthdays
   A. Get presents
   B. Have a party
   C. Am a year older

Now, besides illustrating main ideas and supporting details, the teacher has begun to demonstrate outlining.

After this kind of activity has been done a number of times and the idea of it has been mastered by the children, the teacher can pass out a written paragraph. Together, the teacher and the children can now pull out the main idea and the supporting details. Later, the children should do this kind of activity independently on a worksheet. Of course, individual children and the teacher still need to come together as a group for evaluation of what has been done.

For this activity, as well as all the other activities previously discussed, one or more ESL children in a group probably will be able to give an acceptable response. All the teacher has to do is to elicit that response and ask questions for clarification and extension of what has been said or done.

Summary

The important thing to remember when working with comprehension skills is that much of comprehension is based on an understanding of oral language. Thus, there must be oral communication on as high a level as possible between the teacher and the children, and among the children themselves. Teachers can take time for oral discussion of ideas. They can insist that ESL children speak in complete sentences. They can talk "up," not "down," to children to stretch their vocabulary and understanding. In addition, teachers can encourage those children who have mastered decoding skills to read for pleasure, read for information, read so vocabulary is developed and more elaborate sentence structure is absorbed and understood, and so on. To foster an understanding of language, teachers can provide opportunities for ESL children to hear, speak, and read it throughout the day.

Also, as the use and comprehension of English are extended, the writing abilities of ESL children will automatically be improved. Obviously, children can write no better than they can speak or comprehend. If they cannot use or interpret syntax to convey or understand meaning, they certainly will be unable to write clearly. So in addition to increasing the understanding of what is spoken or read, activities to extend comprehension skills cannot help but enhance writing ability— providing multiple benefits for the classroom time expended.

References

Chomsky, C. "Stages in Language Development and Reading Exposure." *Educational Review*, 1972, *42* (1), 1–33.

Cohen, D. H. "The Effect of Literature on Vocabulary and Reading Achievement." *Elementary English*, 1968, *45* (2), 209–213.

Connor, U. *A Study of Reading Skills among English as a Second Language Learners*. Madison: University of Wisconsin, October 1978. (ERIC Document Reproduction Service No. ED 162 281)

Greenlaw, M. J., Seaton, H. W., and Fisher, C. J. "A Study of Vocabulary and Syntactic Complexity in Developmental First Grade Readers." Paper presented at the Annual Meeting of the National Reading Conference, New Orleans, December 1977. (ERIC Document Reproduction Service No. ED 149 322)

A Vocabulary Building Strategy
for Non-Native Speakers of English

Samuel A. Perez
Northwest Missouri State University

Vocabulary is acquired from experiences a child has and the association of these experiences with words. Some children grow up in homes in which the words, or labels for concepts, they have learned are unique to their linguistic community. In a home where English is not spoken, or where both English and another language are spoken, the child may have learned a Spanish or Chinese word for a concept rather than the English word. In this situation the non-native speaker of English may be handicapped in developing a meaningful vocabulary in English. This child requires special procedures for learning vocabulary.

The emphasis in any vocabulary building procedure should be on meaning, since many non-native speakers of English can pronounce, or decode words, without knowing or understanding their meaning. Generally, this is due to a lack of experiential background which can give meaning to words. The vocabulary building strategy described in this article will help the non-native speaker of English utilize personal experiences in learning how to associate meaning with written language. The procedure will contribute to the student's understanding of ideas presented orally, to growth in expressing ideas in both oral and written form, and to the student's growth in understanding what is read. The procedure can be used with groups of students or individual students at any age or grade level.

The first step calls for the teacher to display a picture, illustration or photograph of interest to students. If working with individual students, the teacher may have the student draw a picture. The picture is used to stimulate a discussion of the objects and actions depicted. The teacher should relate these objects and actions to student experiences.

In the next step the teacher labels the objects and actions in the picture by writing them in manuscript on the chalkboard. Students are then asked to read aloud each word along with the teacher. The students repeat each word without the teacher's help but with the picture to look at if needed. In the next step the picture is taken away and the students are asked to read the words again. If errors are made, the student is shown the picture again. This step reinforces the association of objects and actions in the picture with their spoken and written representations.

The teacher next asks the students to dictate a story suggested by the picture, making use of the words identified in the picture. The students' dictated story is then transcribed onto the chalkboard. Teachers should be sure to use short sentences and as few additional words as possible. After the story has been transcribed, the teacher and students read the story aloud together. The teacher should be careful to move a hand or a pointer under each word as it is read aloud. The students are then asked to read the story aloud as a group and then individually.

The final step of the procedure calls for the teacher to make word cards for the key words from the dictated story. The word cards can be used in the following ways:

1. Students can use the word cards to increase rate of word recognition by recording the time it takes to read all of the words.

2. Students are given several word cards. The teacher gives a definition or clues to the meaning of the word and students read (and/or spell) the word aloud that matches the definition or clues.

3. Students can make sentences with the word cards. The teacher, or another student, can hold up a word card and a student is asked to use the word in a sentence. Or, students can build sentences by putting word cards together.

The vocabulary building procedure described in this article can be effective in promoting the vocabulary growth of non-native speakers of English. The strategy can be successful because it utilizes student experiences in associating meaning with spoken and written words. The procedure exposes the students to the visual images of words, the equivalent pictorial representations, and the spoken representations of words. Any procedure that can assist the non-native speaker of English in vocabulary development will result in a much needed improvement in student confidence and learning.

Contrasting Pairs in the Classroom: One Person's Difference Is Another Person's Lesson

Gregory Larkin
Brigham Young University—Hawaii Campus

As I look over my class roll for freshman English this semester, I see first of all that it is typical of every semester for the past five years, and second, that it is also very unusual when compared to the normal English class anywhere else in the world. The unique feature of my English class is its extreme diversity of students. The thirty-three students in the class are native to the following distinctive cultural groups:

Hawaiian	2	Samoan	6
Mainland United States	3	Tongan	4
Filipino	4	Japanese	3
Chinese	7	Fijian	1
Tahitian	2	Thai	1

Here is a class with only five native speakers of English, and only three of these have grandparents who are native speakers of English. And all of the non-native speakers of English are not even remotely similar in their strengths and weaknesses in the use of the English language. First, they have widely differing learning styles which seem to be somewhat culturally bound. For instance, generally the Oriental students like a methodical, rule-oriented sort of instruction, in which the end product is precisely specified and they write directly to it. The Polynesians, on the other hand, mainly prefer a much more inductive plan, emphasizing a more circuitous approach to the writing task. These basic learning patterns are reflected in the ways the students typically write. The Orientals are typically very good at broad controlling generalizations, but less successful at providing concrete detail. The Polynesians, on the other hand, often write minutely detailed essays which lack any overall thesis or controlling purpose. Of course, these are simply tendencies rather than hard and fast rules that apply in the same degree to every Polynesian and every Oriental. Yet, the basic problem remains—how does one teacher in one classroom teach writing to students with such a wide range of natural styles and such an individual set of problems?

My key to solving this problem has been to form temporary partnerships between pairs of students, whose strengths and weaknesses in a given area are inversely proportional. For instance, to illustrate with the example cited above, if I find a Polynesian who cannot write an effective thesis and an Oriental who cannot provide adequate supporting detail, I assign these two to work as a team on the next essay, but with a special requirement: In this case the controlling purpose would be the responsibility of the Polynesian and the detail would be the responsibility of the Oriental. In other words, each student is responsible for a personally weak area, but the student's working partner is strong in that very area. The ground rules are that the strong student may ask questions or make criticisms in regard to that person's strong area, but may not offer suggestions for revision in that area—those must be done by the student who is weak in that area.

Many different temporary partnerships are formed throughout the semester, depending on the focus being studied at the time, or the particular problem a given student needs to focus on at a given time. For instance, typically, Orientals have much difficulty with individual function words, such as prepositions and articles, but most of them can easily write syntactically mature, individual sentences. On the contrary, many Polynesian students can easily handle function words, but have no idea where an individual sentence begins or ends. In other words, they write fragments and/or run-on sentences. Partners with these contrasting strengths and weaknesses can help each other, with the strong partner in a given area calling the weak partner's attention to a problem area, but not correcting it.

There are many advantages to having students help each other. For one, the teacher is not beleaguered by so many individual problems. The student with problems has somewhere else to turn for help. More importantly, there is a firm and immediate reinforcement of the idea that the student may be weak in one area, but is strong in another. Partners build a genuinely symbiotic relationship, so that no student is put in the situation of dealing only with a teacher, who is by definition always right while the poor student is always wrong. This is a great psychological advantage to the contrasting pairs system.

Also, by having pairs switch often, a great deal of fairly intense interaction occurs among the students themselves, which rarely happens in the traditional lecture classroom or even in the laboratory approach, in which the infallible teacher simply rotates in individual consultation with every student. Many students could get their best insights from a fellow student, but they are often so different that the two never get together naturally. The process of working successfully with a person of a different culture or background is tremendously valuable to every student, especially in this context where no one culture or background is set up as superior, and where one person's strength is another's weakness, and vice versa.

One possible objection to this system is that it seems to presuppose knowledge of each student's strengths and weaknesses on the part of the teacher. In fact, the teacher does need to read a few assignments before suggesting the most effective contrasting student pairs. I deal with this possible problem by inviting students to select their own partners the first few times. Almost inevitably, students select those as similar to themselves as possible and thus teamwork is enhanced in the early going. With their friends, the students become used to the mechanics of working in contrasting pairs while they are still working with someone of their own choosing. By the time they are assigned some partners quite different from themselves, they are used to the system and work comfortably within it.

Although my particular situation is one in which the major differences among students are cultural differences (with related language strengths and weaknesses), the same underlying principles apply and can be put to work among students who differ in ways besides culture— such as intelligence, major interests, physical or emotional maturity. The key points are (1) that every student is different in some way from every other student and (2) that every difference can be linked to a strength and/or weakness in the student's ability to use language. These strengths and weaknesses, if discovered, can be put to effective use, in that every student can have a positive and ego-building experience by teaching others, and every student can learn of personal problems from a relatively nonthreatening "expert." Let me just cite a very few simple examples from the infinite number of possible contrasting pairs that exist in *every* classroom, and in fact in *every* pair of students:

	Partner One	Partner Two	Possible Language Application[s]
Strength	Good grammar	Well organized	Broad outlines
			vs.
Weakness	Poor organization	Poor grammar	Individual sentences
Strength	Good at interpreting sounds of language	Ability to see abstract relationships	Poetic meaning
			vs.
Weakness	Difficulty grasping metaphors	Poor ear for tone	Poetic sound
Strength	Ability to see connection between ideas	Inventive, insightful	Rhetorical invention (generating ideas)
			vs.
Weakness	Unable to think of anything to write about	Unable to see specific relationships	Rhetorical cohesion (providing transitions)
Strength	Sensitive and observant	Confident, able to generate broad insights	Major ideas
			vs.
Weakness	Shy and afraid to assert ideas	Insensitive to fine detail	Specific details

Let me stress, in conclusion, that this system is not offered as a panacea for helping students with difficulties, disabilities, or differences. Obviously, some students have problems that do not contrast meaningfully with any other student's problems. But this system is a way of enriching the students' contact with others, their understanding of their own strengths, and their understanding that their weaknesses are relative rather than absolute. One person's difference is another person's lesson.

The Good News about Newspapers

Chip Shields
Homewood-Flossmoor High School, Illinois

Linda Vondrak
Homewood-Flossmoor High School, Illinois

What's black and white and read all over, costs about ten cents, and is full of fresh ideas every day for teaching English to exceptional students?

A newspaper.

Newspapers have jokes, pictures, maps, graphs, puzzles, and information. So broad is their appeal that we use them in teaching non-native speakers of English, mainstreamed students, and those in remedial reading.

Newspapers are also inexpensive: they can be cut up, written on, and pasted down. And every morning, a bundle of them can be delivered to the door of your school.

Now, some teachers argue that newspapers don't make good teaching tools. They say newspapers are grey and muddy-looking, they're full of ads, and they sometimes carry stories of questionable taste. But how many expensive books, magazines, and filmstrips can match, in terms of high interest, the direct, crisp style of a newspaper's front page? From Benjamin Franklin to Tom Wolfe, journalists have been honing and polishing their prose so that it grabs the reader. Here's a style of writing that goes down easily with mainstreamed students and remedial readers alike. With what economy of style do newspaper writers sum up—in clear, solid English—contemporary issues, problems, and attitudes! In fact, this last quality of newspapers is probably the best thing about them.

Consider the situation of a Vietnamese student, for instance. Many schools have recently experienced an influx of Vietnamese students who speak very little English. Content area teachers often find themselves teaching them because most schools do not have comprehensive programs in English as a second language.

So let's imagine that a Vietnamese student arrives in an American secondary school, having advanced steadily through his own school system. Because he knows almost no English, he's handed a first grade reader and the lesson begins: "Look, look. See, see." All around him are the elements of a sophisticated culture, yet he is relegated to an educational level far below his ability.

Newspapers, however, bridge cultural differences. An exercise that involves putting the frames of a cut-up "Peanuts" cartoon in order is a fast way of introducing such students to American humor. Furthermore, what they can learn from a simple discussion about a political cartoon or a movie ad gives them entree into conversations with their classmates. Just knowing something about current thought will remove, to some degree, the stigma of being a newcomer to this country. Like any young person, a foreign student would rather fit as quickly as possible into a regular program than be kept in a special situation.

A final point about newspapers is that they can be used at different reading levels with students in the same class. The following activities can be adapted at grade level readability for average students, or at a low level for the exceptional student.

Basic Newspaper Activities

    A. Pictures or photographs
       1. Average students: Cut out the caption to a photo that contains a new vocabulary word. Have the student select the correct definition by using the photo and the caption for context clues.
       2. Non-native speaker: Cut out photos reflecting cultural interests. Paste them on cardboard and write words underneath describing what's being shown. Taped auditory phrases on the language master machine can also be used.
    B. Comic strips
       1. Average students: For teaching sequencing skills for improved comprehension, cut apart frames of comic strips and have students put them back in the right order.
       2. Non-native speaker: Repeat the same activity, using "Peanuts" or another strip with few words.
    C. The television guide and weather maps
    Both foreign and average students enjoy locating different areas of the United States on a map. Foreign students especially like comparing local temperatures with those of their homeland. Both kinds of students like identifying television programs and characters.

D. Headlines or titles of articles
   1. Average students: Simple headlines can be cut from articles, taped on paper, and students can then fill in underneath what they think the article might have been about.
   2. Non-native speakers: These students can participate in this exercise, using the simplest headlines possible.
E. Advertising
   1. Average students: Cut out ads and ask questions about prices, items on sale, etc.
   2. Non-native speakers: Students like to look for supermarket ads that help them comparison-shop. This activity also familiarizes students with areas for shopping, and kinds of items available for purchase. Questions about the arithmetic of shopping can usually be asked because most foreign students understand the number system in use here.

4 Students Who Need
Special Challenges

Four Ways to Meet the Needs
of the Gifted Student
in the Regular English Class

Larry Crapse
Florence District One Schools, South Carolina

At some point, each English teacher will encounter in the regular English class a student whose superior intelligence and/or special abilities set that student apart from the others. Some such students flaunt their brilliance; others attempt to hide it to keep from seeming "different" to their peers. Either way, it is the teacher's responsibility to find means of satisfying this person's diverse needs. At least four strategies are available to the teacher who is faced with this situation: developing contracts, designing independent research units, assigning special composition topics, and coordinating activities with mentors in the community.

The use of contracts can be one of the most effective methods of helping a gifted student in the regular class. Before developing a specific outline of activities, however, the teacher should learn as much as possible about the student for whom the outline is to be written. Does the student have a specific academic aptitutde? Is the student gifted in the visual and performing arts? Does the student have remarkable leadership ability? Is the student's thinking creative and productive? What are the student's reading interests and hobbies? These questions can be answered by talking informally with the student, examining the student's cumulative school record, conferring with the parents, or consulting guidance counselors and other teachers who know the student well. In addition, it may be helpful to have the student fill out an interest inventory or write a description of personal interests and goals.

Once this information is gathered, an individual contract can be jointly developed by teacher and students. Individualized lesson plans—with specific objectives, activities, materials, and pre- and post-test items—can be a useful way to help the student avoid boredom with the pace or content of the regular class. The subject matter of the contracts need not be limited to English; the basic language arts skills can be taught, reinforced, and extended through other subject areas. For example, if history is the major pursuit of the student, why not design a contract that requires reading about a particular period or set of events, writing essays or research reports, delivering a speech to a class or club, and listening and reacting to commentaries by noted historians? In this way, the goals of the regular class can be incorporated into an individualized plan, and the student is committed to completion of the assigned tasks by a given date.

An adjunct to the contract method is the independent research approach. Here the student meets with the teacher to decide on a particular problem or topic to investigate. The student must then limit the topic, determine materials and resources to use, estimate the amount of time it will take to complete the project, and determine how the knowledge gained will be shared with the school or community. (This last step is particularly important for students with great leadership ability.) Again, the topic need not be limited to English; math, science, history, or psychology are all valid areas in which the language arts can be correlated. As in the contract method, the student is committed to a set of goals and strategies to be completed by a given date. The main difference between the two methods is in the sharing of information at the end of the tasks: With a contract, the student may simply have the work checked and approved by the teacher, but in the independent study method the goal is dissemination of findings. This can be done through publication and distribution of findings, or presentations to appropriate audiences (classes, school clubs, civic organizations). The school newspaper, PTA meetings, and class newsletters provide excellent forums for such sharing.

A third approach for the gifted is assigning compositions based on the student's special interests and knowledge. While such a method should ideally be used for all students, it is especially effective with the brighter pupil who is easily bored with routine. A student gifted in electronics should be allowed to explain to a layperson how a complicated piece of machinery operates, to elucidate electrical processes, to narrate experiences with wiring, to describe everyday electrical devices (and perhaps their potential dangers) to children, to argue for safe wiring in public buildings and private dwellings, to research various scientists' contributions in electrical studies. Likewise, the student whose major interest is chemistry should be allowed to design, conduct and summarize an experiment; to keep logs and journals detailing technical procedures, to explain to laypersons the significance of the experiment, and to prepare and deliver a speech to an audience of scientists or science teachers. In this approach, too, skills in reading, writing, and speaking are extended while the student engages in fascinating studies.

Finally, one of the best ways to help the gifted is through the use of mentors—professionals or people with special talents or skills. In this approach, the student works with the mentor over a given period of days, weeks, or months and produces a project at the end of the period. For the student gifted in art, a local artist may be of great assistance. For a musically talented pupil, a local musician can be recruited to give one-to-one instruction in composing and performing. For a student with leadership talent, a local civic official can provide on-the-job experience that may be superior to classroom instruction. In all cases, the English teacher can require the student to keep journals or diaries detailing the work, to write essays or research reports on some aspects of the studies, to give speeches to clubs and classes about the experience, and to produce and share an independent project (original musical composition, community survey, painting or sculpture). Many communities are filled with potential mentors who will be delighted to serve in such a capacity.

The implementation of one or more of the approaches presented here does not entail a radical departure from the curriculum required for the "regular" students in English. The gifted should be expected to master the same skills expected of the entire class; the methods of mastery, however, must of necessity be different. Gifted students should also be carefully guided by an understanding teacher in all their efforts, and the teacher should be sure of the backing of the principal and parents as special approaches are used. Rather than pandering to the interests of gifted students, then, these four methods offer creative opportunities to meet their needs. Extension of basic skills, not exclusion, is the foundation of the procedures. In the long run, the students will profit from these experiences.

The Young Author's Project: A Writing Project for Middle School Gifted/Talented Students

Karen Towler
Weldon Middle School, Gladewater, Texas

The criteria for learning activities for the gifted/talented student are often mind boggling. Activities should be product oriented, multi-disciplinary, and individualized as to student interests. They should emphasize creativity as well as the upper levels of Bloom's taxonomy, and should have real-world applications to help instill in the student a sense of responsibility to society—wow!

My problem this year was to come up with writing activities that would meet these numerous and sometimes confusing criteria. My solution was a Young Author's Project.

YAP, as the project was named by the students, was a program I developed in which my sixth grade advanced language arts students wrote and illustrated children's books. Two copies were made of each student's book—one was bound and presented to an elementary school library; the other was submitted to a publisher. The project was a huge success. The kids were enthusiastic and developed a professional concern for their work. After all, they were *real* authors, hoping to achieve publication and earn money for their writing; they certainly didn't want misspelled words in their manuscripts. They became aware of and developed a great appreciation for the many facets of producing a book.

From the time I mentioned it, my students were excited about the prospect of writing children's books. Little did they know what was in store for them. Some offered to turn their stories in the next day. Certainly none of them dreamed of spending ten weeks on the project. When I spoke of submitting the stories to publishers, they became concerned with how to divide their money, and we had to pause for a lesson in royalties, advances, and agents. As I outlined our activities for the project, the students began to see just what a complex task they were taking on.

This is a brief outline of the project:

Step 1: Gathering Information. The students were divided into committees to collect the information that we needed to produce children's books. One committee surveyed children, parents, and teachers as to children's preferences in books; another developed a list of possible publishers; a third gave a report on the publication process and guidelines for submitting manuscripts; still another committee researched and gave presentations on methods of bookbinding.

We all wrote for publishers' guidelines for submitting manuscripts. Outside speakers and field trips added to our store of information. An art teacher advised students on methods of illustrating books. The print shop teacher and students explained layout and the printing process. A writer discussed why and how she writes stories. An elementary teacher spoke on children's interests in books. A reading teacher demonstrated methods for determining readability of a book, using the Fry graph and Dolch word list.

Step 2: Analyzing Children's Literature. Each student read and analyzed several children's books to determine common elements—plots, themes, types of characters, layout methods, types of illustrations—to be able to decide what elements to use.

Step 3: Audience. We discussed the importance of aiming a book at a specific audience. The students noted that a children's book has to please three audiences: publisher, parents, and children. They also noted conflicts in book preferences. For instance, while children love talking-animal stories, most publishers stated that they did not want talking-animal stories submitted to them.

Step 4: Writing and Illustrating Books. Working in pairs of writers and illustrators, the students planned their stories. Each team agreed on the major elements of main characters, setting, and outline of the plot so that each team member could work independently on a part of the book.

Step 5: Revision. After the stories were written and the illustrations were sketched, we came to the most painful part—the revision process. Students shared their stories with parents, children, teachers, and classmates to get their reactions and suggestions. Some rewrote their stories five or six times.

Step 6: Layout. Each writer-illustrator team determined how to position their story and pictures to best appeal to the reader. They wrote the parts of the story for each page on strips of paper and taped them to the corresponding illustrations, rearranging the parts until they achieved the desired effect.

Step 7: Producing Final Copy. When the students were satisfied with their books, they typed or neatly hand-printed (in India ink or with ultrafine-tip markers) the story on heavy drawing paper which they had cut to the appropriate size. The illustrators then drew the final illustrations. In the books to be given to the elementary library, each team included a title page, a biographical sketch of the author and illustrator, and a dedication page.

Step 8: Bookbinding. We made covers for the books by covering cardboard with cloth or adhesive paper. Then we sewed the books together—a task that resulted in many sore thumbs caused by pushing an upholstery needle through the two sheets of cardboard and approximately thirty sheets of drawing paper. Book jackets were made by drawing a design and lettering a title on butcher paper cut slightly larger than the book, then laminating the cover and attaching it to the book with tape.

Step 9: Submitting Manuscripts. A second copy of each book was prepared (according to the guidelines of the publisher selected by the student team) and mailed to the publisher. Then began the long wait for the publisher's response.

After the books were completed, a very proud group of sixth graders held a story hour in several elementary classrooms in our school district, reading the books they had produced. The elementary children were delighted with the stories, many of which were quite good, and they were impressed that the older students had written the books themselves. The local newspaper carried a picture story about the project, and a fine arts club honored the young authors at a meeting. Everyone who saw the books was amazed that 11-year-old kids had written them.

At this point we have received only rejection slips from publishers and naturally the young writers are disappointed. But after learning that Madeline L'Engle's Newbery Award-winning book, *A Wrinkle in Time*, was rejected by more than twenty publishers, the students again submitted their manuscripts with renewed hope.

The Young Author's Project was a real writing experience rather than a mere classroom exercise. I found it perfectly suited to the needs and abilities of gifted/talented students. This project provided my students an opportunity to write for a live audience (children and publishers) and to go through the same excitement, anguish, hard work, and disappointments that any professional writer experiences while producing a manuscript for publication. Students had to examine the business, creative, and technical sides of writing. The project involved complex skills of analyzing the audiences of current books, then using information from many sources to produce an original book, and finally, evaluation of finished products. Each team took ideas for their story from their own interests.

Finally, through the project the students were brought into closer contact with several of their community's children, parents, and civic groups. Their reward for their hard work was a finished product of which they could be proud. The project received excellent evaluations from the students who commented: "I never knew writing was such hard work!" "We did something we could really be proud of." and "Writing the books was good for us and helped the children, too."

Resources

Books

Arbuthnot, May Hill. *Children and Books*. Glenview, Ill.: Scott Foresman, 1972.

Cianciolo, Patricia. *Illustrations in Children's Books*. Dubuque, Iowa: Brown Co. Publishers, 1970.

Hillman, Bruce Joel, ed. *Writer's Market*. Cincinnati: Writer's Digest Books, 1979.

Padgett, Bill, and Zavatsky, Bill. *The Whole Word Catalogue*. New York: Teachers' and Writers' Collaborative, 1977.

Yolen, Jane. *Writing Books for Children*. Boston: Writers, Inc., 1973.

Organizations

The Children's Book Council, Inc., 67 Irving Place, New York, NY 10003.

Films

Creating a Children's Book. Paramount.
Let's Make Up a Story. Coronet.
Story of a Book. Churchill.
Storymaker. Churchill.

Note Worthy: Concise Composition for the Gifted Junior High School Student

Joan Stidham Nist
Auburn University

Note-writing, which has long been an important function in the field of library science, can be adapted to provide the gifted junior high school student with special composition skills. Programs for the gifted usually include individualized reading; these books can provide the material about which gifted students learn to write two kinds of specialized notes.

The first is the evaluative annotation. On the professional level, such annotations serve the book selector in developing library collections. For the gifted student, they can provide an alternative to book reports, one that stresses conciseness rather than elaboration. Typically, the evaluative annotation is about one hundred words long. Within this brief compass, the student is to state characters, setting, and theme; summarize plot; and evaluate the work.

The annotation is headed by basic bibliographic facts: author, title, publisher, year (optional: illustrator, total pages). Repetition of title or reference to "the author" within the note wastes part of the precious word bank. The student soon learns that concrete nouns and active verbs achieve more in the limited space than adjectives, abstractions, and the passive voice. Judgment should be based on comparison with other works and sense of audience appeal. The conclusion can mention deficiency or strength and make a recommendation. Achieving all this in a hundred words will convince the gifted junior high student that writing does indeed make "an exact man."

The second kind of annotation is the "reader's note." Librarians employ this as a way to attract readers to books. Writing the reader's note provides a different challenge of condensation for the student: creating sufficient interest in only thirty-five words for someone to want to read the work. This task can be done in tandem with the evaluative annotation, using the same book; comparison clarifies the differences between the two. First, the reader's note does not evaluate. The selection of a book for notation is implicit acknowledgment that it is worth reading. Second, the plot is not summarized. Rather, specific episodes intrinsic to the action are featured; atmosphere is highlighted. Only enough is said to create suspense; the climax is not disclosed. Even the bibliographic heading can be truncated to basic author-title form.

The reader's note can provide literary sport for gifted junior high school students. The books represent a literary carnival; each student writes as barker for a book-booth, trying in thirty-five words to coax in readers. Collected reader's notes from a class of gifted students can form a home-produced "selection aid" volume to place with NCTE's booklists *Your Reading* and *Books for You*. The notes, whether on large cards or paper, can be decorated with hand-drawn pictures, photographs, or cut-out magazine illustrations, and placed in ring binders accessible to schoolmates.

A spin-off skill for gifted students who gain competence in writing annotations can be their enhanced reference use of bibliographical guides made up of such concise reviews; for example, the *Junior* and *Senior High School Library Catalogs*. Having learned to write with brevity and precision, they will be better able to discriminate competent synopsis and critical analysis in their reading.

Computer Sound Poems: An Exercise in Writing Surrealistic Poetry for Gifted Student Writers

Deanna M. Gutschow
Whitefish Bay High School, Wisconsin

Can verbally gifted students be taught some important basics of good poetry writing and still have fun at the same time? My experiment with "computer sound poems" convinces me that they can.

The idea for this assignment came to me last winter when I was teaching poetry writing to a group of ninth graders enrolled in a special English class specifically designed for gifted student writers. (The Whitefish Bay Public Schools Gifted Writers Project is being developed with the assistance of an ESEA Title IV-C Innovative/Exemplary Grant.) We had begun the unit by looking at how sensory images were used in various poems by students and professional poets, and then the students read a chapter on the sounds of English in John Frederick Nims's excellent text on poetry writing, *Western Wind, An Introduction to Poetry* (Random House, 1974). In discussing that chapter, I pointed out how the high vowels in Dylan Thomas's "Do Not Go Gentle into That Good Night" create a feeling of intensity that reinforces the meaning of the poem, while the low, resonant vowels which predominate in Robert Frost's "Once by the Pacific" contribute to its somber, reflective tone.

The students listened dutifully to my comments, but it was obvious from the lack of expression on their faces that they were hardly "turned on" by what I had to say. The winter doldrums were upon them, and they were clearly more interested in daydreaming about Christmas vacation—only a week away—than in concentrating on sound patterns in poetry. I was afraid that if I gave them a poetry writing assignment so close to vacation, the results would be perfunctory and uninspired. Yet at the same time I wanted them to work with sound as a poetic device instead of simply reading what other poets had written. That was when the idea for computer sound poems hit me like a well-aimed snowball.

The next day I walked into class with a box of scissors and a stack of small envelopes instead of the poetry text. Ignoring their quizzical looks, I handed out a scissors and an envelope to each student and told them to take out a sheet of paper and a pencil.

I then divided the class into two groups, A and B, and said, "I want each student in Group A to make up a list of ten adjectives, ten nouns, ten verbs, and five adverbs. The adverbs can be any words that indicate 'when,' 'where,' or 'how.' Each of these thirty-five words should contain, in a stressed syllable, one of the low vowels (as in *boo!, bone, book,* or *bought*) or one of the lower middle vowels (as in *boy, bough, bar,* or *bud.*)" I also told them that they should try to select soft-sounding words, containing "musical" consonants like *l, w, y, r, m, n, b, p,* and *f,* rather than those containing harsher sounds like *k,* or the *gr* combination.

Turning to the students in Group B, I told them to make up the same kind of list, except that they were to use words containing the high vowel sounds (as in *buy, bay,* and *bee*), or the higher middle vowels (as in *bird, bat, bet,* and *bit*). The consonants they were to emphasize in their words were the fricatives *(h, f, v, th, dh, s, z, sh, zh)* and/or plosives *(p, b, t, d, k,* and the hard *g).*

I urged all students to make up lists of interesting, unusual words, or words in which sound echoed meaning. At this point the students did not yet know what would happen to their word lists, but, their interest aroused, they set to work with considerable enthusiasm— rummaging through dictionaries and textbooks for words, sounding various words out loud, and laughing at each other's choices.

Near the end of the period I told the students to cut out their words so that each word was on a small rectangle of paper, and to put these rectangles into the envelopes I had given them. I then had the students write their names on the envelopes and indicate whether their words contained high or low vowels so that I could group the envelopes on that basis.

The next day, I formed groups of three or four students and handed each group three or four envelopes of words, making sure that no students received their own envelopes. Thus, each group ended up with a total of 105 or 140 words, depending on the number of people in the group, and their sets of words contained either all high frequency vowels or all low frequency ones, rather than a mixture of both. At this point, I explained what the students were supposed to do with the words:

"Now that you have a random collection of words containing either low or high vowels," I said, "I want you to function like computers that have been programmed with certain word lists and syntactic patterns and can therefore generate meaningful, if somewhat unusual, poetry. You are to arrange these words into sentences that form a poem, a poem which may be highly unconventional in meaning, but which still has logic to it, is clear and coherent."

After that I laid out the ground rules for writing the poems. First, the students could not add any new nouns, verbs, adjectives, or adverbs to the group of words they had, but they could change the form of a word (*run* to *running* or *runner,* for example), and they could use one part of speech as some other part of speech (*rain* as an adjective, for example). Second, they could add any "structure" words they wanted—like prepositions, conjunctions, determiners, and subordinators—in order to create meaningful syntactic relationships among the words. Third, they could use the same word more than once in their poem, if necessary. I also reviewed with them the importance of line arrangement and reminded them that they should use the end of a line or the end of a stanza as a position of emphasis.

Thus, the computer sound poem assignment was intended to force students to create sense out of non-sense, using syntax, line arrangement, sound patterns, and, I hoped, a sense of humor. Only after they had completed their poems did I talk about surrealistic poetry and how the surrealists had tried to jolt their readers out of habitual ways of perceiving and thinking. And when the students read a number of surrealistic poems, including "Zeppelin" by Andrew Glaze, and "What the Violins Sing in Their Baconfat Bed" by Jean Arp (From Nims's *Western Wind*), they realized how similar those poems were to their own computer sound creations.

But when I first told my class what they were supposed to do, they protested that the assignment was impossible. It was only after I firmly set them to work, arranging and rearranging the words on their desk-tops, that they began to get into the spirit of the project. Within minutes, the room was abuzz with enthusiastic noise as students sounded out lines and laughed over the zany images that were beginning to emerge from the random groups of words before them.

I should add that, later in the period, when one group told me they very much wanted to use a word they didn't have, I let them borrow that word from another group. But I kept such borrowing to a minimum, allowing only three additions per group. Most groups, however, did not have to resort to this.

My suspicion that the students thoroughly enjoyed this assignment was confirmed by their behavior when they completed their poems during the next two class periods. Instead of simply handing in the completed poems, each group insisted on reading their poem out loud to me, making sure that their manner of reading emphasized the resonant quality of the lower vowels or the shrillness of the high ones. And on the last day of class before Christmas vacation, when all the groups had finished their poems, they actually begged me to let them do the assignment again!

The examples of computer sound poems which follow make clear that students not only worked skillfully with sound, syntax, and line arrangement, but also exploited their capacity for playfulness and imaginative thought. They had learned a great deal about writing poetry, but they had also had fun.

The Groovey Frog

The groovey frog haughtily hopped,
  smoking
      a cool
          oblong
             cigar.
His yacht suddenly BLOOMED
  from the gloom.
His rude clone showed up,
  fooling the oyster, hog and fowl of the crew.
Those stupid frogs knuckled each other,
  lunging,
  clawing,
  throwing stones.
A sober crocus thoughtfully thrust them
    both
into the horrid water.

The moral of this story is—
  NEVER KNUCKLE
  OR
  CLAW YOUR CLONE.

Leigh Nystrom
Judy Polacheck
Daphne Rubert

The Swooning Moon

The moon swooned,
and slowly tongued a tune,
low and soft,
but the shore was stubborn
and wouldn't move.
The lone moon boomed,
shooting the hour down, slowly,
into the cold, lovely pool.
"No," croaked the homely nun,
the gong is down, and alone."

Angie Hoffman

The Blue Baboon of the Zoo

The young blue baboon—
surrounded by sounds and balloons,
thought to void his exposure with enthusiasm.
He cautiously slaughtered a cruel clown
    who fought the foul fool.
Evasively zooming, the baboon soon shot a loon
    and stole one hundred balloons.
A lawyer found a blood puddle;
    rude war closed in.

Karin Loberg
Carla Kocher
Tom Schmid

The Mighty Prisoner

Hair of gray, he is mistaken
    for a zebra. He eyes the key,
grasping for it. Swiftly he flies
    to freedom in the pitch-dark.
He eats peanuts and green veggies . . .
    and shuffles, leaps and runs
    through a muddy stream,
        gaily preaching
    creatively written prayers of the sea
    and of rainbows, bright in the sky.

He spies the mayor
    acting in an amphitheater,
    playing an angry dictator,
and approaches him,
    crying and pleading for freedom.

Meeting this creepy, hairy criminal
    made the mayor shudder meekly
        and arrange an invitation
            for the criminal
                to bake pastries.

John Melvin
Linda Miller
Katie Rutigliano

The Clown

Clouds softly float past
   a turquoise moon
as a maudlin clown moves slowly,
    his golden shoes possessing thoughts
      of yesterday.

The clown
   now openly hopes for tomorrow
    to smile on him.

Peggy Dooley
Vita Foldi
Chacha Azcueta

Rhetoric: The Qualitative Difference —A Writing Program for Gifted and Talented High School Seniors

Judith Barnett
University of Texas at Austin

Planning an advanced placement writing class for gifted and talented students poses several problems for teachers who want to help these youngsters develop as thinkers and writers. First, while these youngsters are unusually effective in spoken expression, many dislike refining their ideas in writing. The second problem arises from the level of competence as writers that they have already achieved. They are able to crank out "school writing" without any real intellectual engagement with their subjects. Writing for them is an imitation of communication.

Thus the challenge to the teacher is to provide a program qualitatively different from the usual twelfth grade writing curriculum. This means that the students will at once focus on how they function as writers as well as develop a more sophisticated understanding of the composing act. They will employ consciously an expanding repertory of rhetorical strategies.

Achieving this goal means going beyond the materials in the standard high school texts, which continue to ignore developments in rhetorical theory, particularly invention, as well as the research now available supporting a new conception of the composing process. Teachers of gifted and talented students will find the content and practice they need in the work of rhetorical theorists who have concerned themselves with teaching as well.

In developing a writing course for high school advance placement seniors, I have borrowed from the work of Frank D'Angelo (1975), Francis Christensen (1968), James Kinneavy (1971), James Moffett and Betty Wagner (1976), and Richard Young, Alton Becker, and Kenneth Pike (1970). The unit in narrative writing that this article describes is the first in a series of three units devoted to topics grouped according to their logical relationships: narration, process analysis, and cause and effect. Each unit in the series requires approximately two weeks. Some class periods are devoted to reading and discussion; others are designated as writing labs with the emphasis placed on writing in a less structured environment.

The unit in narrative writing focuses on invention and introduces systematic methods for generating material to write about. The unit also introduces stylistic choices in sentence structure, the cumulative sentence and the free modifier.

By way of introducing new ways of looking at familiar subjects, the class begins the tagmemic discovery procedure by considering how people "chunk" experience in recurring patterns: birth, coming of age, marriage, old age, and death. For the young, some of the rites of coming of age might include being confirmed, making a debut, or taking the driver's license test. These chunks can be viewed as systems with sub parts or as being themselves part of larger systems. The experience of taking the driver's test is made up of many sub units: filling out forms, waiting one's turn, meeting the examiner, the moment of putting the car into gear and driving out to begin the test, and so forth. However, the driving test is for many the first signal received from the adult world that the individual is advancing toward adult privileges and responsibilities. As such, the driving test becomes part of a larger system or chunk of experience called coming of age. Furthermore, people focus on these chunks of experience in different ways. Thus an account of a driving test might shift from peripheral focus—a sidelong glance at the examiner, gauging his reactions—to a nuclear focus on the candidate— clammy hands on the steering wheel, ice cold sweat trickling between the shoulderblades, a sick feeling of apprehension. Then the observor would choose which focus required more complete development. Finally, the chunk of experience can best be understood in terms of its contrastive features, its range of variation, and its distribution in a larger context. Students might ask themselves what specific features make one person's driving test unlike any other person's. How much could this experience change and still remain the same? Some examples for generating discussion on this point might be: an experienced driver taking the test for an international license; a friend taking the test for the second time, having failed it once before; a younger brother or sister, the "baby" of the family, taking the test for the first time. Considered in a larger context, what is the importance of the driving test to the individual taking it? Is getting a driver's license comparable to coming of age in the United States? Is this really a recognition of maturity or admission to adult status? Is it parallel with coming-of-age rites in other cultures?

With these questions in mind, students read and discuss several essays employing narrative as the method of development, asking themselves what the writer is implying about human experience. They consider why using narrative as the method of development in a particular piece of discourse is effective. They look at the unit of experience and the interrelationship with the focus that the writer has chosen. What aspects of the unit has the writer chosen to emphasize? Or, has the writer chosen to view the experience as part of a larger system? Has the writer done both?

Two essays that I have used successfully to stimulate this type of discussion are E. B. White's "Once More to the Lake" (1965) and Bruce Catton's "The Joy Above the Stars, the Terror Below the Ice" (1972). In each essay, the writer uses personal experience in order to draw universal truths. For White, revisiting a lake where he had spent many boyhood summers, this time in his young son's company, not only recreates the pleasures of the past, but provides a signal of mortality. Catton also draws on boyhood experiences to reflect on exaltation and terror existing together, each the obverse of the other in accepting what life offers.

For writing warm-ups, we attempt "chaining," described by Moffett (1976), first stringing a series of incidents elicited by certain associations and then using the tagmemic discovery procedures to analyze the components of the experience. Then students begin developing incidents for themselves, using the tagmemic procedure to generate material and then shifting focus and selecting the aspects of the incident requiring elaboration given that focus. Students write the most promising incident, first as an interior monologue emphasizing the observer's perceptions and feelings, and then shifting the focus. In the first instance, instead of merely reporting, "I was scared," one student analyzed the components of the feeling and wrote "My heart was pounding, my hands shaking so that I could not fit the key into the lock. Hours passed before the lock turned and the door finally opened." Another student, describing a visit to her grandmother, wrote, "The lights were all out and the curtains were drawn. The only sounds came from her breathing, and the ticking of a clock over the mantle of the fireplace. The clock ticked loudly, and the sound seemed to echo as if the room were hollow." In each case the emphasis is placed on including those details relevant to the reader's understanding of the experience. These trials are shared with a partner for immediate feedback. Usually they are rewritten several times, incorporating the increased perceptions.

Drawing on what students know about plot structure from their study of fiction, the class considers how writers build suspense and emotional intensity into narrative and they then attempt to incorporate these elements into their own narratives. Looking at plot structure, they ask themselves if they are structuring their own narratives logically to build to the crisis. Do their narratives develop in emotional intensity? What options are open to them with the focus that they have chosen?

The culminating activity is a writing assignment in which students draw from their experience an incident which provides an insight into human nature that can be generalized. The students use the discovery procedures which they have been practicing, generating content by systematic questioning, looking for the features of the experience. After writing a narrative that they feel provides enough relevant details for understanding the experience, students write a conclusion elaborating on the resulting insight. Then they give consideration to the introduction, examining the ways in which a writer sets the mood and prepares the reader for what is to follow. Students work on appropriate introductions for their narratives, selecting details that set the tone and project the ideas that the essay will develop.

The path does not lie as smoothly as this description might seem to suggest. One problem that must be dealt with in revising is the way in which descriptive and narrative details may be added to sentences without making them unwieldy. Some exercises taken from Christensen's (1968) cumulative sentence and the addition of free modifiers help solve this problem.

Christensen first offers a professional model:

> In his room Cal sat at his desk,
>   elbows down,
>   hands holding his aching head together,
>   palms pushing against the sides of his head. . . .
>
> John Steinbeck

Then he provides a student exercise: "As the light turned green, he drove away," (additional visual detail) (additional nonvisual detail).

The student using the exercise provides one additional visual detail and one nonvisual detail using the absolute, a free modifier with its own subject and predicate. Note that an absolute does not have a complete verb in the predicate. Verbal elements and attached complements and modifiers form the predicate of the absolute.

The suggested response to the student exercise is:

> As the light turned green, he drove away,
>   his shoulders gradually relaxing,
>   the radio filling the air with the sounds of the Top Ten.

When the narratives have been completed, committees of students select the best essays in their groups, and these are published for the class. Those students who wish their writing to remain private place their final efforts in their folders. I read and respond to each essay, and any essay may be resubmitted for further response or assessment when the writer has attempted a substantive revision.

This unit in narrative writing has been successful in all of my classes. Students tell me that this writing is satisfying and furthermore, that they have learned more about writing from this assignment than from many others. This affective response is heartening, but equally important for the teacher is the increased awareness of the writer's options in the composing process that students develop, and their proficiency in using those options. It is this increased awareness of the rhetorical situation that constitutes the qualitative difference in this writing course for gifted and talented twelfth grade students.

References

Christensen, Francis. *The Christensen Rhetoric Program, The Sentence and the Paragraph*. New York: Harper and Row, 1968.

D'Angelo, Frank. *A Conceptual Theory of Rhetoric*. Cambridge: Winthrop Publishers, Inc., 1975.

Kinneavy, James. *A Theory of Discourse*. Englewood Cliffs, N.J.: Prentice Hall, Inc., 1971.

Moffett, James, and Wagner, Betty Jane. *Student-Centered Language Arts and Reading, K-13*. 2nd ed. Boston: Houghton Mifflin Co., 1976.

Young, Richard E., Becker, Alton L., and Pike, Kenneth L. *Rhetoric: Discovery and Change*. New York: Harcourt, Brace and World, Inc., 1970.

Works Cited

White, E. B. "Once More to the Lake." *The Norton Reader, An Anthology of Expository Prose*. New York: W. W. Norton and Co., 1965.

Catton, Bruce. "The Joy Above the Stars, the Terror Below the Ice." *Waiting for the Morning Train*. New York: Doubleday Co., Inc., 1972. Excerpt also appeared in *Family Weekly*, December 30, 1973.

This Is Just to Say It Works

Sheila A. Lisman
Hutchinson High School, Kansas

"Are we gonna study poetry?"

"I hate it!"

"We won't have to write any, will we?"

I couldn't believe it! In a class designated for gifted and talented juniors, I never expected to hear this. I thought they would be vitally interested in poetic expression and the symbolic significance of . . . .

In "average" classes there is nothing quite like the announcement of the poetry unit coming on the heels of a trudge through *Ethan Frome*, but instructors of honors classes can be somewhat surprised by the negative reaction their students have to poetry. As a result, I developed some clandestine activities that have lured students into enjoying and writing poetry.

Now on a fair March day I stand excitedly by the door and pass out sheets with the following poem on them. (I make no mention of poetry, however, and since even gifted students think all poetry rhymes, many don't recognize this as "poetry.")

> This Is Just to Say
>
> I have eaten
> the plums
> that were in
> the ice box
>
> and which
> you were probably
> saving
> for breakfast
>
> Forgive me
> they were delicious
> so sweet
> and so cold
>
> William Carlos Williams

As I hand them the poem, I merely indicate that they are to try to write one like it. Here are some student versions:

I have caught
the fly ball
that you hit

which came close
to sailing over
the big red fence

Forgive me
this could have been
the winning hit

I have
interrupted the
life you would
have had together

I bet you
didn't expect me
to come along
in the deal

Forgive me
if I happen
to be my
father's daughter

I detonated
your mom
and her cat
also her chair

she is old
and probably
was going to
die soon anyway

Forgive me
though because
the cat
was worth money

The process of imitative writing is not new. In *I Never Told Anybody: Teaching Poetry Writing in a Nursing Home* (New York: Random House, 1977), Kenneth Koch showed his students "simple forms." He did this, as he stated, so that "between the writer and the poem were no difficult demands of rhyme, meter, rhetoric, diction or subject matter." Later, encouraged by their success, he used "bolder forms." According to Koch, he used the poetry of such poets as D.H. Lawrence, Walt Whitman, and William Carlos Williams.

As the students write their versions, we type them and place them on the bulletin board immediately. Reading the cards, the students note "cleverness" without my help. There is also unprompted revision.

The following day we read "Chicago" from their text. After the reading, I ask them to write their version titled "Hutchinson." They jump at this. It seems to satisfy their pseudo-sophisticated contempt for the good old home town. The opening of one went:

> Cultural armpit of the world,
> redundant, waster of time,
> player of the lousy top 40,
> idiotic, salt shaker for the world
> city of old folks' homes

While this wouldn't impress the Chamber of Commerce, students are involved. By now some think poetry writing is "easy," so it is time to use a subtle model such as Langston Hughes's poem "Suicide's Note."

> The calm
> cool face of the river
> asked me for a kiss.

For a few gory moments we review various ways to end it all, and they are off.

> I spun the
> cylinder and was
> shocked to find the
> bullet.

> The cliff
> was steep enough
> for an evening drive.

> The neat
> coil of the rope
> wanted me for its knot.

Things are going well, so I have begun to brag in the teachers' lounge. I actually have to explain that students are crowding into my doorway to read their poetry on the bulletin board. (Some of my colleagues assume it's to see dirty graffiti—cynics!)

Since contrast plays an important part in poetry, I next use a model by Hutchinson-born William Stafford.

Vacation

One scene as I bow to pour her coffee:—

> Three Indians in the scouring drouth
> huddle at a grave scooped in the gravel,
> lean to the wind as our train goes by.
> Someone is gone.
> There is dust on everything in Nevada.

I pour the cream.

Here are two student poems:

Chore

One scene as I lean over the sudsy water:—

> The lonesome figure
> struggling against nature,
> plowed on through
> a cold, covered world,
> a world not unlike the one
> found in a child's paper weight.

I dry the dish.

School

One scene as I walk down the hall:—

> The principal has another boy
> cowering in the corner by the radiator,
> leaning on the wall as if for protection.
> It is of no use.
> He is carted away.

I go on to gym class.

Since many gifted students enjoy writing parodies, I suggest they do one of Stephen Crane's "The Heart."

> In the desert
> I saw a creature, naked, bestial,
> Who, squatting upon the ground,
> Held his heart in his hands,
> And ate of it.
> I said, "Is it good, friend?"
> "It is bitter, bitter," he answered.
> "But I like it
> Because it is bitter
> And because it is my heart."

The student who wrote the following poem used a different creature.

The Cow

In a pasture
I saw a creature, known as a cow,
Who, cooling in a pond's mud,
Was biting its cud.
To the cow I said, "What are you chewing?"
"My cud," answered the cow.
"I'm bored, and there's nothing to chew.
But, alas, my cud has calories too!"

"The Short Night (III)" translated by Harold G. Henderson gives students an opportunity to indicate the results of their "short nights."

The short night is through
on the hairy caterpillar
little beads of dew.

Student versions:

The short night is through:
deep dark bags shadowing
eyes which are looking at you.

The short night is through
the sleeping turtle dove
and its mourning coo.

Although the students are imitating the same models, there turns out to be great diversity in their poems. Each teacher can find a variety of poems which will make successful models.

These exercises should not be viewed as an end in themselves but should be seen as "warm-ups" for any poetry exploration a teacher wants to do. The exercises described above took an enjoyable four days. Gifted students gained confidence and set out to find their own models; the exercises led others to pursue ideas of their own. Since the imitations do not have to be done to the letter (or syllable), students are free to exercise their creative powers. Yet they realize poetry writing does require discipline, and the value of disciplined creativity is a good lesson for gifted—and less gifted—students to learn.

Note:

This Is Just to Say

I have cheated
and used
this idea
with the average

you were probably
wondering what
to do with them

Forgive me
but I meet
120 students
every day

Postscript: Yes, I must make a confession. While I tailored these exercises to students with special abilities, other students saw the examples and became interested. So they did the same things. "They" includes about ninety other students typical of the heterogeneous grouping found in any public high school—several learning disabled students, a number reading below grade level, and this year a special challenge, a class of twenty-three "macho men" who considered poetry "queer" (in every sense of the word!).

Interestingly enough, some of the most creative poems were written by other than designated "gifted" students. Of the poems printed in this article, only three were written by "gifted" students.

DATE DUE